Praise for *Spir...*

Dr. Mathew is both a teach... ...
of doing, and he does ministry based on his teachings.

This book is basic yet profound at the same time. It is based on basic biblical and timeless theological truths; yet it contains deep, profound insights. This is exactly what every minister needs to be effective in the twenty-first century. In the sea of books written for Christian leaders, this book stands out! Many books are appetizers or desserts, but this is the main course. I would highly recommend this book to every pastor, leader, and Bible school student.

Rev. How Tan, Senior Pastor, Heart of God Church, Singapore

Today, perhaps more than ever, the role of church leadership is to devote our time and effort—our hearts—to seek and find the true leader of the church, the Holy Spirit, and allow Him to be the front and center in every aspect of the church and ministry. *Spirit-Led Ministry in the 21st Century* is a blueprint for ministry that desires to have an eternal impact in people's lives. This book highlights the why and the who of ministry—which is the reason each one of us were called to give our lives in the first place. *Spirit-Led Ministry in the 21st Century* calls us back to a place of relying on the partnership of the Holy Spirit to accomplish that for which we've been apprehended.

Rev. Steve Boyce, Senior Pastor, New Life Church, Rhode Island, USA

Having more than four decades of experience in a globally impacting ministry, Dr. Thomson K. Mathew gives the reader a broad perspective of biblical, theological, and practical ministry. He provides some essential tools that are necessary for a sound, dynamic, and Spirit-empowered ministry. This is a timely book and an excellent manual for every church builder in the twenty-first century.

Rev. Bugvi Olson, Minister, The Keldan Church, Faroe Islands

In his book *Spirit-Led Ministry in the 21st Century*, Dr. Thomson Mathew combines his eminent academic knowledge in the pastoral field and a long life of both pastoral practice and charismatic ministry. Few people internationally have this combined experience, and I give his important book my best recommendations.

Dr. Anders Gerdmar, President, Scandinavian School of Theology and Associate Professor of New Testament Exegesis, Uppsala University, Sweden

The book titled *Spirit-Led Ministry in the 21st Century* is a timely book emerging out of a brilliant academician, passionate pastor, and a seasoned practitioner with an honest dependence on the power and guidance of the Holy Spirit. The book is well crafted and blends the three most essentials for ministry, which are biblically grounded, theologically comprehensive and sound, as well as practically relevant. Dr. Thomson K. Mathew aims to impart this priceless tool to learners and practitioners of ministry, reminding them of the importance of the role and the involvement of the Holy Spirit in the ministry. These three essentials were established with ample biblical models, metaphors, and encounters ... Therefore, this book is an excellent tool that provides practical insights for students, professors, pastors, and missionaries, both those who are confused about a call of God and others who are sure of God's call to ministry. It is a must-read book for all Christians.

Rev. Biren Kumar Nayak, Vice Principal, New Life College, Bangalore, India

The twenty-first century is characterized by the fourth industrial revolution and globalization. People today are living in totally different social contexts than before. However, the minister of the gospel is still called to do the work of ministry—preaching, teaching, healing, and leading the people. Since Dr. Thomson Mathew has served the Lord in various ministerial positions as pastor, chaplain, professor, seminary dean, evangelist, and conference speaker at various international contexts (including Korea), he is one of the rare scholars who can write on this subject with conviction and authority. One distinction of this book is his approach to ministry from the Pentecostal/Charismatic perspective. We can find terminologies such as inspirational, Spirit-filled, empowerment, healing, signs and wonders, miracle, etc., very often in this text. Without the leading and guiding of the Holy Spirit, no one can successfully do the work of ministry. Chapter three is totally devoted to studying the work and role of the Holy Spirit in ministry, which we cannot find in any other books. Dr. Mathew and I worked together for more than two decades in training Korean pastors through the Doctor of Ministry program at Oral Roberts University. His teaching in the classroom as well as in conferences has impacted many Korean pastors. This book will help pastors and ministry students everywhere serve the Lord and the saints better.

Dr. Yeol Soo Eim, Former President and Professor, Asia Life University, Taejon, Korea

Spirit-led Ministry in the 21st Century is a very practical and comprehensive book on Christian ministry. Biblical, theological, and practical aspects of Christian ministry are well presented in this book. One outstanding mark of the book is its emphasis on the role of the Holy Spirit in ministry. How we should give freedom to the Holy Spirit in all the various aspects of ministry such as evangelism, discipleship, preaching, teaching, healing, and organizing is explained with clarity and authority. A solid historical foundation of Christian ministry given in the book is a special asset. Special emphasis has been given to the concept of servant leadership. This will be a very useful handbook for leaders who are engaged in ministry to families, women, children, and so on. Having served as a teacher of seminary level courses in Christian ministry for more than two decades, I can say for sure that most of the syllabus areas of the Christian ministry courses are well covered in this book. I strongly recommend *Spirit-led Ministry in the 21st Century* to theological students and Christian ministers.

Rev. Saju Joseph, Director, India Bible College and Seminary, Kerala, India

SPIRIT-LED MINISTRY IN THE TWENTY-FIRST CENTURY

Spirit-Empowered Preaching, Teaching, Healing, and Leadership

REVISED AND UPDATED EDITION

THOMSON K. MATHEW

WESTBOW PRESS®
A DIVISION OF THOMAS NELSON
& ZONDERVAN

Copyright © 2017 Thomson K. Mathew.
www.thomsonkmathew.com

All rights reserved. No part of this book may be used or reproduced by any means, graphic, electronic, or mechanical, including photocopying, recording, taping or by any information storage retrieval system without the written permission of the author except in the case of brief quotations embodied in critical articles and reviews.

All Scripture quotations, unless otherwise indicated, are taken from the Holy Bible, New International Version®, NIV®. Copyright ©1973, 1978, 1984, 2011 by Biblica, Inc.™ Used by permission of Zondervan. All rights reserved worldwide. www.zondervan.com The "NIV" and "New International Version" are trademarks registered in the United States Patent and Trademark Office by Biblica, Inc.™

Scripture taken from the New King James Version®. Copyright © 1982 by Thomas Nelson. Used by permission. All rights reserved.

Scripture taken from the King James Version of the Bible.

WestBow Press books may be ordered through booksellers or by contacting:

WestBow Press
A Division of Thomas Nelson & Zondervan
1663 Liberty Drive
Bloomington, IN 47403
www.westbowpress.com
1 (866) 928-1240

Because of the dynamic nature of the Internet, any web addresses or links contained in this book may have changed since publication and may no longer be valid. The views expressed in this work are solely those of the author and do not necessarily reflect the views of the publisher, and the publisher hereby disclaims any responsibility for them.

Any people depicted in stock imagery provided by Thinkstock are models, and such images are being used for illustrative purposes only. Certain stock imagery © Thinkstock.

ISBN: 978-1-5127-9231-7 (sc)
ISBN: 978-1-5127-9232-4 (e)

Library of Congress Control Number: 2017910228

Print information available on the last page.

WestBow Press rev. date: 7/31/2017

To

Molly
Amy, Fiju, Philip, and Joseph
Jamie

Contents

Foreword to the Second Edition xiii
Foreword xv
Introduction xvii

Chapter 1   Defining Ministry 1
   A Biblical View 1
      Biblical Metaphors 4
      Jesus's Model 5
      Jesus the Pastor 7
      Pre-Ministry Encounter 8
   A Theological View 9
      Hope-Bearing 10
      God's Messengers 11
      Ministerial Authority 13
      Kingdom of God 14
      Sacred Vocation 16
      Revealing God's Heart 19
   A Practical View 19
      Ministry as Leadership 20
      Ministry as Relationship 22
      Incarnational Presence 22
      Ministry as Memory 23
      Contemporary Images 26
   Rewards of Ministry 28

Chapter 2 Ministry: A Historical Perspective 30
    General Story of Christianity 30
    A Brief History of Ministry 32
    The Particular Story of Shepherding 36
        Church Fathers on Pastoral Work 37
        Pastoral Care during the Middle Ages and
           Pre-Reformation Period 41
        The Reformers and Pastoral Ministry 41
        Pastoral Work during Post-Reformation Period 44
    Ministry in America 45
        The Evangelicals 46
        Pentecostal-Charismatic Ministry 47
        A Thematic History 49
        Impact of Dominant Social Characters 51
        Positive Ministry Trends in the New Century 54

Chapter 3 Ministry and the Holy Spirit 56
    When the Spirit Came 58
    Ministry Practices in Acts 61
    Understanding Empowerment 65
        Power and Powerlessness 67
        Love and Power 68
        Revelation and Risk 69
        Poverty and Prosperity 70
        Authority of God's Son 71
        Authority of God's Word 74
    A Spirit-Empowered Church 75
        Caring and Meeting Needs 77
        Evangelizing 80
        Seven Forces 81
        A Strategic Proposal for Evangelism 84
        Making Disciples 87

Organism and Organization 88
Under Authority and Accountable 91
Portrait of a Healthy Congregation 92

Chapter 4 Empowered and Competent Ministry 98
Competent Ministries 99
Ministry to Families 99
Ministry to Women 102
Ministry to Children 105
Institutional Ministry/Chaplaincy 107
Praise and Worship Ministry 110
Continuing Education of Ministers 114
Why Continuing Education? 115
History 116
Needs 117
Resources 118
Being Healthy in Ministry 120

Chapter 5 Preaching in the Power of the Spirit 124
Eight Preaching Principles 128
Spirit-Led Interpretation of the Bible 134

Chapter 6 Teaching As Jesus Taught 138
Jesus, Teaching, and the Holy Spirit 139
Educational Philosophy 140
Good Teaching 142
Adult Education 143
Teaching Teens 146
Teaching for Daily Decisions 149
Types of Faith 151
Theological Reflection 152
Church as a Theological Seminary 155

Chapter 7 Healing Ministry in the New Century	158
Faith and Healing	161
Signs and Wonders	163
Evangelistic Versus Pastoral Healing	165
Theological Presuppositions	166
Healing Ministry in the Local Church	169
Chapter 8 Empowered Servant Leadership	172
Next Stage of Leadership	173
Biblical Language of Leadership	174
Secrets of Success	175
Management and Conflict Resolution	176
Limits of Ministry Leadership	178
Effective Leadership	178
A Spirit-Led Model	180
Encounter with God	182
Anointing of the Holy Spirit	183
Walk by Faith	185
Chapter 9 Becoming a Spirit-Empowered Minister	188
A Call to Ministry	189
A Call to Empowerment	194
A Call to Excellence	197
Notes	203
Bibliography	211

Foreword to the Second Edition

Ministry is no easy task. Ministry leaders are keenly aware of the complexity of ministry and their dependence on God's power and leading to effectively execute His calling for their lives. Without the divine dimension, the minister sooner or later exhausts her or his own resources and skill sets. Thankfully, the Spirit of God empowers the minister for the tasks at hand. Dr. Thomson K. Mathew seamlessly weaves the practices of ministry together with Spirit empowerment in this text.

Dr. Mathew writes as an insider to the Spirit-empowered movement. He grew up in the Pentecostal tradition and served for decades in a university institution marked by the Charismatic renewal of the latter half of the twentieth century. These traditions grew exponentially in the twentieth century and have influenced all corners of the Christian world today. In the twenty-first century, the Holy Spirit has become mainstream. Furthermore, postmodernism's emphasis on experience as bearer of truth contributes to the marginalization of cessationism and fosters a longing to be Spirit-led in ministry. In this second edition, Dr. Mathew uses the language of Spirit-empowered ministry throughout the text in a way that speaks effectively and contextually to today's ministers.

The multifaceted role of the minister is attested to by the breadth of scripture. While the *shepherd* metaphor for the minister reverberated meaning in an agrarian world, it does not speak with such clarity in the twenty-first century. Even its translated equivalent, *pastor*, remains vague in today's world. The various Christian traditions and subcultures each conceptualize ministry leadership differently, complicating our understanding of what the minister does. Dr. Mathew carefully unpacks the complex role of the minister for the reader. In the pages of *Spirit-Led Ministry in the 21st Century*, the reader gains a robust understanding of ministerial identity and function for today's world.

Dr. Mathew is a pastor's pastor. I have known him for nearly two decades and can attest to both his reservoir of ministry wisdom and his caring pastoral heart for all those he encounters. Students love his wisdom, colleagues seek out his counsel, staff treasure his loving care, congregations are captivated by his preaching, and all see Jesus in his character. Fifteen years ago, he spoke words into my life that served as a rudder as I sailed out into the deep waters of church planting. "Remember," he said, "you are planting an orchard, not a cornfield." I clung to those words of truth during the following ten years of church planting. In the pages of this book, the reader will discover keys to cultivating a ministry orchard that produces fruit year after year.

John Thompson, DSL
Director of the Doctor of Ministry Program
Graduate School of Theology and Ministry
Oral Roberts University
Spring 2017

Foreword

Currently there is a plethora of books, journals, and magazines dealing with the subject of the role of a pastor including preaching, teaching, healing, and leading. Most of these books are written by leading evangelical ministers. Their works are well done and insightful, but often underemphasize the Holy Spirit's work in these roles.

There is a great need for information on ministry from a Pentecostal/Charismatic dimension. This book by Dr. Thomson Mathew meets that need. Here is a well trained and experienced Pentecostal/Charismatic pastor, chaplain, and theological educator writing out of years of experience about roles of the minister with a balanced emphasis. We now have a textbook quality guide to add to the current offering of books on the subject. This book is both academic and practical at the same time.

Undergirding Dr. Mathew's four major roles of a minister are two strong foundational stones—character and skills. In Psalm 78:72 we read, "And David shepherded them with integrity of heart; with skillful hands he led them." These twins of balance are found in each of the roles delineated by Thomson Mathew. In fact, he practices this balance in his own life and teaches them by his example. Really, what good are skills if they are not accompanied by character of heart, and how effective is a person with character minus skills?

This book is both cutting edge and basic. May its truths impact all readers in an ever changing and sometimes dangerous world, one that desperately needs Spirit-empowered ministers with integrity (character) and skills.

Kenneth Mayton, EdD
Graduate School of Theology and Ministry
Oral Roberts University

Introduction

For a number of years now, I have felt the need for a book on Spirit-empowered ministry that is biblically sound and theologically balanced. While there are plenty of books on ministry and various specialized ministries, there is a real shortage of books on ministry from a Spirit-filled perspective. Most books on ministry do not pay adequate attention to the role of the Holy Spirit in ministry. And many of them seem to neglect the church's ministry of healing.

I have been teaching courses in ministry and pastoral care at Oral Roberts University Graduate School of Theology and Ministry for nearly three decades. My students kept asking me to put into writing some of the material I have been teaching. Being the dean of a college and seminary, there never was a convenient time to do so. Finally, I came to the conclusion that there never would be an ideal time and started to put a collection together. I first produced it more than a decade ago as a class reader for my students titled *Spirit-Led Ministry in the 21st Century*. A generous sabbatical I received during the 2016–17 academic year has made it possible for me to revise and update that work to produce this volume.

This is meant to be an essential reader and a practical guide on Spirit-empowered ministry for anyone currently engaged in ministry or contemplating ministry. I hope ministers and ministry students in all faith groups will read these pages as I have sincerely attempted to present a theology of ministry that is faithful to the Bible and open to the empowerment of the Holy Spirit in this volume. I have also focused on the four major things Jesus asked His followers to do—preach, teach, heal, and lead. I have presented these topics in light of the challenges posed by the twenty-first century.

I have not written an original treatise. In addition to my own observations, these pages contain ideas I gleaned from many people—family members who are ministers, several teachers and mentors, and a number of authors I have read. Additionally, I owe much to the theological faculty at Oral Roberts University, whose outlook on ministry is reflected here. We have spent countless hours in the last few years discussing and debating what biblical ministry ought to look like today. We have argued about what a Spirit-led minister—the intended product of our seminary—should be like. I want to express my deep gratitude to these colleagues, especially to those who participated in the lunch room table talks on a regular basis.

I am indebted to several individuals who made this work possible. My wife, Molly; long-term administrative assistant, Judy Cope; and editorial assistant, Marlene Mankins, are among them. I am also grateful to President William M. Wilson and Provost Kathaleen Reid-Martinez of Oral Roberts University for granting me a generous sabbatical.

Probably my strongest qualification for writing this book is that I am a third-generation minister within the Pentecostal/Charismatic tradition whose ancestors were Saint Thomas Christians of India. My father and grandfather were Pentecostal preachers in South India. My wife's father and grandfather were also Pentecostal ministers there. My father-in-law pastored one church for forty years in Kerala State, India. My father pastored his last church for thirty years as he supervised thirty other churches in his district.

My brother and my wife's brother are pastors. All four of my sisters are married to pastors. I grew up in parsonages in India until I came to America in 1972. After my studies at Yale Divinity School, I pastored a local church in New Haven, Connecticut, for five years before becoming a chaplain and professor. All these relationships, experiences, and observations have influenced this writing.

At my father's funeral service a few years ago, I spoke about our family's self-understanding by making reference to the conversation between Joseph's brothers and the Pharaoh in Egypt: "Pharaoh asked the brothers, 'What is your occupation?' 'Your servants are shepherds,' they replied to Pharaoh, 'just as our fathers were'" (Gen. 47:3). We are also a family of shepherds and this book is written from the perspective of a shepherd. I hope it will be seen as a special strength of this work.

The modern Spirit-empowered movement is more than a hundred years old now. The pioneers of the movement faced their day and finished their course. I believe that the movement needs more well trained leaders with passion and competence who can address the challenges of their own day. I have accepted the preparation of such ministers as the calling and mission of my life. This book is a humble contribution toward that mission.

If a current pastor or future minister receives an insight or a sense of encouragement by reading these pages, I will be more than grateful. I submit these pages to God for His purposes.

Thomson K. Mathew
Graduate School of Theology and Ministry
Oral Roberts University
Tulsa, Oklahoma, USA
Spring 2017

Chapter 1
Defining Ministry

> He appointed twelve that they might be with him
> and that he might send them out to preach and
> to have authority to drive out demons.
> —Mark 3:14–15

What is this vocation called ministry? How is it different from contemporary helping professions? Is it really unique among the professions? Responding to these questions may be a good place to start a book on Spirit-empowered ministry. Since ministry can be viewed from biblical, theological, and practical perspectives, let's begin this discussion with a biblical definition of Christian ministry.

A Biblical View

Since Christian ministry must be guided by its biblical mandates at all times, it is appropriate to begin with the scriptural texts. First, Christian ministry is a total response to God's call on a person's life (2 Tim. 1:9; 1 Thess. 2:12). While the Bible acknowledges the priesthood of all believers, it clearly indicates that God calls certain individuals for specific offices of ministry. In *The Purpose of the*

Church and Its Ministry, Richard Niebuhr outlines four distinct calls in the life of a minister.[1] The first is the call to become a Christian. Everyone receives this call, but the future minister receives an additional secret call. This is one's inner sense of a calling that is not shared by anyone else. This secret call is followed by a providential call that voluntarily manifests itself through God-given gifts and talents. Finally, the minister receives what Niebuhr calls an ecclesiastical call that publicly acknowledges God's call on his or her life. In this stage, God's call is publicly affirmed by the body of Christ and may be confirmed through ordination.

Scripture defines ministry as being a coworker with God, carrying out His purposes in the world (John 4:34; 2 Cor. 6:1). The almighty God chooses to depend on fragile human beings to complete His work of restoration, reconciliation, and redemption in this fallen world. Ministry is, therefore, doing God's will in the world. Before God's will can be carried out, it must be sought in prayer. Ministry, then, is seeking God's will in prayer and doing His will through one's life (1 John 2:17).

Ordained ministers are not expected to carry out all of the practical aspects of ministry. God gave apostles, prophets, evangelists, pastors, and teachers for the equipping of the believers to do the work of the ministry, according to Ephesians 4:12. To a large degree, ministry is simply equipping and enabling other believers to fulfill the multiple ministries of God's church. The ultimate purpose of ministry is, therefore, to produce people who minister. Although not all are called to the offices of ministry, all believers are called to minister. True ministry is enabling others to serve in the name of Jesus by edifying, equipping, and helping them to grow.

Ministry involves bringing men and women into a vital relationship with God through Jesus Christ (2 Cor. 5:20). It is also the proclamation (*kerygma*) of the gospel of Jesus Christ (2 Tim. 4:2, 5). As people are reconciled with God, they are also called to become reconciled with one another; therefore, one can say that biblical ministry is a relational enterprise involving the work of reconciliation.

Scripture confirms that ministry is bringing wholeness to individuals: "May your whole spirit, soul, and body be kept blameless at the coming of our Lord Jesus Christ" (1 Thess. 5:23). According to this text, biblical wholeness is holiness. God calls His broken children to wholeness and holiness; therefore, ministry must seek to restore persons to wholeness by bringing healing to body, mind, spirit, and relationships.

True ministry can only be accomplished through a life of servanthood to God and others in the name of Christ (Gal. 5:13, 6:2, 5). *Diakonia* means service. The highest title in the kingdom of God is that of servant; thus, leadership in God's church must be servant leadership.

Scripture also emphasizes the importance of *koinonia*, the fellowship of believers and the communion of saints (1 John 1:7). Ministry involves facilitating this fellowship and communion in the body of Christ.

In essence, ministry is the call of God on one's life. A minister is a gift of God to the church (Eph. 4:11), and he or she is a representative of God who pleads with the world to be reconciled with God (2 Cor. 5:18–19). A minister, as an ambassador, must dialogue with the world while at the same time remaining in constant communication with God. The pastoral epistles list other ministerial duties, including reproving, rebuking, exhorting, enduring, and doing the work of an evangelist. They also include equipping, perfecting, edifying, unifying, and bringing persons to maturity.

Biblical Metaphors

The Gospels are filled with images of ministry and discipleship. David W. Bennett, in *Metaphors of Ministry*, categorizes these as images of people and images of things.[2] Some images are relationship oriented, while others are task oriented. Relationship-oriented images include those of brother, sister, child, son, friend, guest, and disciple. According to Bennett, images of servant, manager, shepherd, worker, apostle, witness, and fisherman are primarily task-oriented metaphors. Scripture uses commonplace things such as soil, field, firstfruits, vine and branches, wheat, sheep, salt, light, building, and body to bear the image of ministry.

From these images Bennett draws certain metaphoric themes. First, he sees the theme of weakness and dependence in biblical ministry. Ministers are weak vessels on their own, but they can depend on God for strength. Bennett sees a second theme of honor and dignity in biblical ministry. It is an honor to be a minister of the gospel; God calls His children to be vessels of honor, and they bring glory to God when they serve honorably. Bennett also sees the theme of interconnection in biblical ministry in images such as branch, building, and body. Ministry involves connecting people to God and connecting people to people. Ministers connect people in a disconnected world, which makes ministry a vocation of inclusion rather than exclusion.

A minister fulfills many roles. Functionally, he or she participates in the community and engages in doing the many life-giving tasks needed within the community. Regardless of his or her position, a minister is a person who serves under authority; the minister has authority, but he or she is not to become authoritarian. Ultimately, a minister is called to identify with Jesus in the pattern of His life, and the minister is accountable to Christ for his or her character and service.

Jesus's Model

Christian ministry is the continuing legacy of the ministry of Jesus of Nazareth. Jesus was an apostle of God, and He came to proclaim and inaugurate the kingdom of God. An apostle is one who is sent. The Father sent Jesus, and Jesus sent twelve envoys. We are to receive Him and those whom He sent. "Let us go ... That is why I have come" (Mark 1:38). Scripture tells us that those who received the disciples also received Jesus: "He who receives you receives me" (Matt. 10:40). Ministry is the work of those who are sent by Jesus.

Jesus was the ideal servant, fulfilling the biblical prophecies of the suffering servant. The disciples were to follow His example of servanthood (John 13:5); they were not to "lord it over" others (Matt. 20:25–28). Among His disciples, the greatest one was to become the servant of all (Matt. 23:11).

Jesus's ministry was powerful because of the presence and power of the Holy Spirit in His life. Jesus was conceived by the Spirit (Matt. 1:20, 23). The Holy Spirit came upon Him at the time of His baptism (Mark 1:8–11), and the Spirit drove Him to the wilderness to be tempted (Luke 4:1). He returned from the wilderness in the power of the Holy Spirit (Luke 4:14) to carry out His ministry (Mark 13:11; Matt. 10:20; Luke 12:12; John 14:15–17, 15:26). Jesus promised the outpouring of the Holy Spirit on His disciples (Luke 24:49); their ministry was to be characterized by the empowerment of the Holy Spirit. The Spirit was to enable them to speak (Mark 13:11), to testify, and to bear witness. Jesus—the apostle, the servant, and the one who was led by the Spirit—was the ministry role model for His disciples, and He remains the same for all who will follow their example.

Mark the evangelist presents the essence of ministry as he outlines Jesus's ministry: "He appointed twelve—designating them apostles—that they might be with him and that he might send them out to preach and to have authority to drive out demons" (Mark 3:14–15). Performance of ministry tasks was of secondary importance to the primary call of the disciples *to be with Jesus*. The disciples were called to preach and to drive out demons, but being with Jesus was their first priority. They were set apart to be with Him first and then to set the captives free.

In his book *Renewing Our Ministry*, David McKenna describes the relationship between the minister and Jesus Christ, stating that Jesus Christ calls His ministers to be trustworthy, teachable, and task oriented.[3] According to McKenna, Christ is the model of trustworthiness and the mentor who teaches truth. Christ is also the enabler of His followers who imitate Him as partakers of His divine nature.

Christ is the mentor who calls His disciples to be teachable teachers, says McKenna, and the one who calls them to be task oriented. Ministry includes the tasks of leading and managing. Leadership focuses on effectiveness, so a good leader ensures that the correct tasks are carried out. A manager's focus is on efficiency, ensuring that the tasks are accomplished in a productive manner. A leader articulates a vision, and the manager implements it.

A Christ-centered ministry, as with all leadership, involves tasks as well as relationships. The tasks of ministry relate to the mission and ministries of the church. The primary mission of the church is to evangelize (Matt. 28:18–20) and make disciples (2 Tim. 2:2). The ministries of the church include worship (John 4:24), preaching (2 Tim. 3:16), teaching (Matt. 28:20), healing (Matt. 10:8), prayer (Eph. 6:18), and fellowship (Heb. 10:23–25). The ordinances (1 Cor. 11:23, 24; Mark 16:16) of the church are part of worship. All these ministries require careful management, which involves prayerful planning, organizing, leading, and assessing.

Jesus the Pastor

Jesus is the best model of a pastor-shepherd. In *Jesus the Pastor,* John W. Frye identifies the characteristics of Jesus as a model shepherd.[4] Jesus had a strong sense of identity; He knew who He was and what He was called to do. This sense of identity enabled Him to focus on His destiny and purpose. Significantly, Jesus did not depend on His ministerial performance to settle His identity; His father affirmed Him before He performed the first miracle, saying "You are my Son, whom I love; with you I am well pleased" (Luke 3:22). Jesus's identity was not performance-based; rather it was rooted in Father God. Many ministers fall into the trap of performance-based identity, but a biblical model of ministry is anchored in God and in His call on the minister's life.

The Spirit of the Lord was upon Jesus to preach the good news. He was the incarnational presence of God to the degree that those around him could say, "We beheld His glory." As a shepherd He had a compassionate heart; He went about His Father's work, ministering to the oppressed. He was spiritually disciplined, committed to a community, and willing to tell the truth at all costs. He was not afraid of the devil, but He took the power of evil seriously. He also shared authority with His disciples; He knew that sharing His authority did not diminish it.

Pre-Ministry Encounter

The Bible clearly illustrates that an encounter with God is a prerequisite for authentic life and ministry. Abraham, the father of all who believe, had an encounter with the living God (Gen. 17:1–6). Similarly, Moses experienced a powerful encounter with God (Ex. 3:1–7). Moses trained Joshua, but prior to the commencement of Joshua's leadership, he also had an encounter with God.

> After the death of Moses the servant of the Lord, the Lord said to Joshua son of Nun, Moses' aide: "Moses my servant is dead. Now then, you and all these people, get ready to cross the Jordan River into the land I am about to give to them—to the Israelites ... As I was with Moses, so I will be with you; I will never leave you nor forsake you." (Josh. 1:1, 2, 5)

Samuel, the great Old Testament prophet, had an encounter with God while he was still a child (1 Sam. 3:4). He heard God's voice when the sons of Eli the priest did not. The Word of the Lord came down to Elijah (1 Kings 17:2) and launched him into a great ministry of service to God and His people. Elisha also heard the Lord (2 Kings 7:1). Isaiah encountered God in the year King Uzziah died (Isa. 6:1). He had a glimpse of God's holiness, which confronted his own inadequacies, causing him to cry out, "Woe to me." Isaiah experienced the touch of God's fire and responded to His call, "Whom shall I send? And who will go for us?"

Individual encounters with the divine continued to occur in the New Testament as a prerequisite of ministry. Saul of Tarsus, for example, encountered the living savior and experienced a transformed life; the persecutor became a preacher of the gospel.

An encounter with God that gives a sense of calling is a definite requirement of successful ministry. An individual does not call him- or herself; he or she is called by God; his or her responsibility is to respond. Moses argued against His call, but God won the argument. Jonah tried to run away from God's call, but God won the race. God is still calling today. The harvest is ripe but the laborers are few; those who have heard God's call must respond.

A Theological View

Most contemporary theological writings lack the supernatural aspect of Christian ministry, but a New Testament model of ministry embodies Spirit-empowered preaching, teaching, healing, and leading. Christian ministers are called to do something beyond their own abilities, and they need the empowerment of the Holy Spirit to accomplish it. Christian ministers cannot afford to be like other helping professionals because they must deal with the natural as well as the supernatural aspects of life. This is why efforts to narrow ministry down to leadership, management, counseling, and so on have failed miserably in the past.

Christian ministers cannot afford to neglect the prophetic aspect of ministry due to their concern for order as the church leadership has done many times in the past.[5] They represent God and are called to do His work. This work cannot be done without the empowerment of God's Spirit. It is better for a minister to come to terms with this reality as early as possible in his or her ministry.

Looking at ministry from a theological perspective will be helpful at this point. Let's begin with the premise that Spirit-empowered ministry, first of all, is hope-bearing.

Hope-Bearing

A Spirit-empowered minister is a person filled with the Holy Spirit and called by God for His purposes. This is an individual who is in dialogue with God and people at the same time, his or her ministry embodying his or her identity as a disciple of Jesus Christ. A Spirit-filled minister must have congruence and integrity in his or her life. A person is congruent when he or she practices what he or she preaches. He or she has integrity when his or her word can be trusted. Integrity is an indicator of hope.

A Spirit-led minister must seek to be both a reflective practitioner and a grassroots theologian, one who allows his or her actions to be guided by the Holy Spirit and by personal reflection on the Word of God. The Word, the Spirit, and the community of faith provide the authority and the balance he or she needs. A Spirit-led minister is attuned to the Spirit of God through an ongoing dialogue with God. He or she is able to instill hope in others because he or she has personally experienced God's saving and healing power in some form. The Spirit-filled minister is willing to test all things by the Word of God and reject those things not affirmed by God's Word. It is crucial that this individual cares deeply for others.

A minister will be identified by the message of hope that he or she conveys. I recall growing up in a parsonage in Kerala, India, where merchants sold all types of produce from door to door. Salesmen came to the door and announced their wares, then moved on to the next house. My grandmother sometimes missed the salesman and had to call after him. She would call him by whatever he was carrying on his head to sell, such as "Mr. Banana" or "Mr. Coconut." Of course, these were not the names of the merchants, but they always responded because they were identified by what they were carrying. A minister is a bearer of hope; he or she is identified as a hope-bearer. "Christ in you is the hope of glory" (Col. 1:27).

God's Messengers

The Old Testament prophets and New Testament apostles are often viewed as role models for ministry. Ministers, as carriers of God's message, can also follow the model of Gabriel, the angel who served as a special messenger for God. Listen to his words to Zechariah the priest:

> I am Gabriel. I stand in the presence of God, and I have been sent to speak to you and to tell you this good news. And now you will be silent and not able to speak until the day this happens, because you did not believe my words, which will come true at their proper time. (Luke 1:19, 20)

Gabriel, as a messenger for God, described his ministry to Zechariah as: (1) standing in the presence of God, (2) being sent to speak good news, and (3) waiting in expectation for the fulfillment of God's Word.

Ministry involves all three aspects of Gabriel's work—standing, speaking, and waiting—yet the hardest tasks are standing in the presence of God to hear His Word and waiting for His timing when the Word is fulfilled. The Bible uses two different Greek words for the concept of time. The word *chronos* denotes chronological or ordinary time, whereas the word *kairos* represents God's time or the fullness of time. Ministry demands that we patiently wait for God's timing in all things.

Delivering God's message is not risk-free. A minister who shares God's Word risks not only the rejection of that word by the hearers, but also the possibility of that message not being fulfilled within one's own time-frame or as one expected. For example, the prophet Isaiah gave a word from the Lord to King Hezekiah concerning the king's impending death. The prophet clearly heard from God and was faithful to share what he heard. Hezekiah, however, repented, and God extended his life. It appeared that the prophet's initial word did not come to pass. Because God is sovereign, the Christian minister lives with the double risk of his message being rejected in the first place, and then not being fulfilled as expected.

Since God is not confined to humankind's time or space, His work often involves times and seasons that require much patience. For example, Jonah did not want to go to Nineveh, but through unusual circumstances he eventually delivered the message God gave him to the citizens of Nineveh. In spite of his initial reluctance to follow God's call, Jonah was faithful at last to deliver the word he received. When the people responded to Jonah's message, however, "God ... had compassion and did not bring upon them the destruction he had threatened" (Jon. 3:10). Jonah was frustrated by this, but he learned that the nature of ministry involves being faithful to God and His Word without taking offense at the consequences.

Time spent in God's presence and hearing His Word results in satisfaction rather than frustration. Most often ministers are bearers of good news that does come to pass. They have the privilege to say that the blind will see, the deaf will hear, and the lame will walk. They can also encourage the weak to say, "I am strong," and the poor to say, "I am rich." Ministers can exhort the hurting, knowing that the Lord's desire is to bring healing and wholeness to all people. Ministers must simply trust God when occasionally the good news they deliver may sound like bad news.

Moses was commissioned as he stood in the presence of God on Mount Horeb. Samuel heard God's strategic plan in His temple.

The minister of the gospel is a herald who receives direction in God's presence. Ministers should strive to follow the model of Gabriel the messenger, being faithful to stand (hear), speak, and wait patiently.

Ministerial Authority

Any attempt to define ministry must address the concept of ministerial authority. What is the source of a minister's authority? What model of authority should he or she adopt? Individuals often imitate models of authority found in the business world and the military, yet a minister is to follow Jesus's model of authority. Jesus did not disclaim His authority (Luke 4:32), but made it clear that His authority came from God and therefore did not conform to the lower authority of this world (John 8:28).

> Jesus called them together and said, "You know that the rulers of the Gentiles lord it over them, and their high officials exercise authority over them. Not so with you. Instead, whoever wants to become great among you must be your servant, and whoever wants to be first must be your slave—just as the Son of Man did not come to be served, but to serve, and to give his life as a ransom for many." (Matt. 20:25-28)

His authority made Jesus a servant. All authority was given to Him, but Jesus imposed limitations on how He exercised that authority (Matt. 4:1-11, 20:20-28) and willingly shared His authority with His disciples.

A minister's authority, according to Niebuhr, comes from God's call.[6] According to Samuel Southard, the sources of authority for a minister are obedience to God's call, the lordship of Jesus, the church—the body of Christ—and legal charge.[7] Southard also states that ministerial authority manifests itself in five different ways: prophetic, evangelistic, pastoral, priestly, and organizational.[8] Godly character confirms a minister's authority, since character is formed in a person as he or she submits to authority. The centurion in the gospel understood this mystery. He had authority because he was under authority. Similarly, a minister of the gospel has authority because he or she is under authority. Paul exhorts ministers, "Follow me as I follow Christ."

Kingdom of God

Christian ministry must be seen in light of Jesus's teaching on the kingdom of God. John the Baptist came announcing the arrival of the kingdom, and Jesus proclaimed that it had arrived, saying, "Repent, for the kingdom of heaven is at hand" (Matt.3:2, 4:17 NKJV). John was beheaded and Jesus was crucified, but the disciples took up the same message of the kingdom (Luke 9:1–6). The New Testament illustrates that the preaching of the kingdom continued through the apostles, as seen in Paul's ministry (Rom. 14:17).

The kingdom has three dimensions of time. In one respect, the kingdom of God has already come as Jesus announced (Matt. 4:17; Luke 10:8, 9). Scripture states that the kingdom of God is a present reality (Luke 17:21). The kingdom of God also has a cosmic future dimension that has not yet fully been realized. The kingdom of God is a mystery according to the parables of Jesus, and it operates on a unique value system. For example, in the kingdom, giving is the way to receive (Luke 6:38), and the last becomes the first (Mark 10:31):

> If anyone would come after me, he must deny himself and take up his cross and follow me. For whoever wants to save his life will lose it, but whoever loses his life for me and for the gospel will save it. (Mark 8:34, 35)

In the kingdom, dying is the way to live, and losing is the way to gain.

In terms of the kingdom of God being a mystery, Jesus uses the examples of a mustard seed and yeast to represent the kingdom of God as a living organism that grows. As the mustard seed grows into a tree in which the birds of the air come to perch, and as the yeast spreads throughout a batch of dough, so the kingdom of God must increase (Matt. 13:31–33). God allows good and bad to coexist in His kingdom, just as good seeds grow with the tares (Matt. 13:24–26). The Master allows the weeds to remain for a season, "Because while you are pulling the weeds, you may root up the wheat with them" (Matt. 13:29). But a day will come when the weeds will be tied up in bundles to be burned, and "The angels will come and separate the wicked from the righteous and throw them into the fiery furnace, where there will be weeping and gnashing of teeth" (Matt. 13:49–50). The kingdom is also like a fisherman's net pulled up on the shore, full of good fish along with bad ones. The kingdom of heaven will also be like ten virgins who took their lamps and went out to meet the bridegroom; five of them were foolishly unprepared for His coming, but five of them had wisely prepared.

The kingdom of God is a powerful entity. God reigns in His kingdom, and the kingdom's power is derived from the King. The resources of the kingdom may not always manifest in silver and gold, but the name of Jesus always holds power. Christian ministry is kingdom work, and as a citizen of the kingdom, a minister has access to the power and resources of God's kingdom. The book of Acts demonstrates the manifestation of the power of the kingdom of God over and over again. This book chronicles the power of God, the power of His Spirit, the power of holy living, and the power of holy giving. We are admonished to seek God's kingdom first; all other things shall be added to us (Matt. 6:33).

The kingdom of God may not always appear attractive from the outside; in fact, it may be deceptively unattractive. A person who finds a piece of land with a treasure hidden in it goes and sells all he or she has in order to buy that field. A merchant looking for fine pearls finds one of great worth and sells all of his or her possessions in order to acquire it (Matt. 13:44–46). The behavior of these people makes no sense to outside observers, who wonder what they could possibly have found that would cause them to give up all that they have. Yet for the people who made the transaction the answer is clear: They have found treasure beyond description. This is the true picture of a Christian minister. Observers of a minister in his or her culture may not understand or appreciate what all the excitement is about, but the minister goes on, comprehending something unspeakable and full of glory.

Sacred Vocation

Eugene Peterson, the pastor who authored the *Message* version of the Bible, articulated the vocation of pastor in a very moving way in his autobiographical book, *The Pastor: A Memoir.*[9] Born to a butcher father and a Pentecostal preacher mother, Peterson was lured away by God's call from a prestigious academic life to become a pastor of a local church. In his vivid description of that journey, Peterson makes many vital observations regarding pastoral ministry. I highly recommend his insights to contemporary pastors who are being tempted to go for the glitter and glory of unbiblical leadership models and strictly professional ministerial performance.

The current culture demands leaders who can get things done and make things happen. Many Bible colleges and seminaries are guilty of buying into this idea without critique. Christian media are also guilty as they promote performers rather than true pastors. Certainly pastors must also be doers, but according to Peterson, if pastoring is reduced to simply performance, we are losing the essential element of being a pastor, which is to watch over the souls of men and women, to care for them, and to pray without ceasing.

Pastors are not created by seminaries; God makes pastors. It is the call of God that makes one a pastor. There are some now in pastoral positions because they have certain skills, but having no calling, they wind up making the congregation of the people of God their audience and marketplace.

Personally, I do not believe that there is anything wrong with adapting useful ideas about organization, leadership, or communication for the sake of the gospel. The problem is accepting them without biblical scrutiny and adopting those that are contrary to the spirit of the Word of God just because they work. I am not suggesting that we abandon all methodologies of ministry just because they are not directly mentioned in the Bible. What I am saying, as Peterson has so eloquently done in his volume, is to go by the Word of God. Peterson is right. Pastors are not called to be bureaucrats. Their main job is not management. Primarily they are shepherds who pay attention in the name of Jesus to people who live their lives in these perilous times.

Churches are meant to grow naturally because they are living organisms. This growth is supposed to happen through conversion of people in response to the Body of Christ bearing witness to the transforming power of the gospel. Stealing sheep as the mode of church growth is not biblical. Churches are not supposed to be in competition with one another, fighting for a fair share of the religious market.

Peterson makes many interesting observations. Churches are not franchises, he says. Pastors must preach the Word that their people need to hear, not just preach about the furniture in heaven and the temperature in hell. Jesus Christ and Him crucified should be the topic.

Peterson is very hard on the modern church growth movement. He may be overstating the case, but his warning that there are three intoxicators that tempt pastors—wine, women, and crowd—is very interesting. He feels that "crowds are a worse danger" because "size is the great de-personalizer." Peterson is calling the church to return from the entertainment business back to the edification work.

Pastors should not have major control issues. They should not manipulate people. They must care for the people and do all they can to create a culture of hospitality in their churches. A church should be a place where relationships are primary, a place of hospitality. Pastors must live with the awareness of their own mortality. They die daily, but also live daily with the anticipation of the resurrection. "We practice our death by giving up our will to live on our own terms. Only in that ... are we able to practice resurrection," says Peterson.

Reading Eugene Peterson's memoir brought back many memories of my own parents and grandparents. They toiled in the hills and plains of South India, finished their work, and went home to be with Christ. Informed by the Word of God and nothing much more, they lived out their vocation of being shepherds to people of modest means. They loved them and cared for them. They extended their own lives and resources unselfishly to hurting people for the sake of the kingdom of God. That model of pastoral ministry scared me as a child, but also drew my attention. Having been a pastor and teacher, I now recognize more fully the importance of the vocation I witnessed as a child in my family of shepherds.

Revealing God's Heart

In summary, ministry is more than preaching, teaching, counseling, soul winning, or healing. It is more than performing various tasks, including even Spirit-led signs and wonders. Ministry involves an individual embodying the incarnational presence of Christ in a fragmented world, in obedience to God's call and in accordance with His will. In many ways ministry is simply revealing the heart of God. In order to minister effectively, one must dialogue with God and humankind at the same time. Ultimately, ministry is faithfulness to God, who calls men and women out of darkness into His marvelous light. Perhaps Paul's testimony before King Agrippa regarding the Lord's instructions to him on the fateful day he journeyed to Damascus summarizes God's heart regarding ministry: "I am sending you to them to open their eyes and turn them from darkness to light, and from the power of Satan to God, so that they may receive forgiveness of sins and a place among those who are sanctified by faith in me" (Acts 26:17–18).

A Practical View

Having looked at Christian ministry from biblical and theological perspectives, let us now turn to a practical view of ministry. Ministry is defined practically in multiple ways. Henri Nouwen stated that ministry involves teaching, preaching, counseling, organizing, and celebrating.[10] Victor Furnish said that ministry is monitoring, maintaining, and strengthening the community of faith, as well as *koinonia* (fellowship), *eucharista* (celebration), and *diakonia* (service).[11] There are several ways of looking at the actual practice of ministry. First of all, Christian ministry is a special form of leadership.

Ministry as Leadership

A minister is a leader of God's people, called and formed in a particular way. In this regard, Moses is a fine example of a minister in leadership. Moses clearly led God's people, God Himself having chosen him to lead them. Eight distinctive leadership characteristics are evident in Moses's life and ministry:

1. Hearing God: Moses was a man who had a listening ear for God's voice. From the time he heard the voice coming out of the burning bush, Moses continually desired to hear God. Even when God's message was stern, Moses listened to it carefully.
2. Obeying God: Listening to God is very different from obeying Him. Moses was not only a listener but also an obedient servant of God. Moses followed God's directives very closely, with the exception of one occasion. As a leader, he represented God and implemented His wishes among the people. Although people were often offended, Moses gave priority to God's opinion of him.
3. Confronting Evil: Moses was not afraid to confront evil. He was willing to look the oppressor in the face and command him to let God's people go. Human power did not intimidate this man of God. He knew that the Egyptian leader could destroy his body, but not his spirit.
4. Correcting the Saints: Moses was willing to correct the saints when they needed correction. He rebuked and disciplined them as needed, because he knew that he served a holy God whom he wanted his people to please.
5. Interceding for the People: Moses implemented rough discipline because in his heart he was a caring shepherd. He had to be both prophet and priest at the same time. As

prophet he told the people, "Thus saith the Lord"; as priest he cried out before God on behalf of his people by standing in the gap for them.
6. Being Human: Many leaders try to act as if they are very different from their people. Some act as though they are spiritually superior and have a secret chat line to God that others do not have. Unfortunately much of this spiritual superiority is not authentic. Moses was a man of God, but he remained human before his people. The glory of God was on his face, yet he lived his daily life among the people as a human being. He experienced emotions of happiness, sadness, and anger, like any other human being, but he knew he was their leader, and the people knew it, too.
7. Mentoring Others: Many leaders are self-absorbed and shortsighted, assuming that they will be present to lead forever. Moses was different. He mentored others in leadership by training them to assume leadership in the future. He wanted to ensure that there would not be a leadership vacuum after his death. Many present-day organizations experience a leadership vacuum when people have not been mentored in leadership.
8. Developing Anointed Leaders: Moses shared responsibility and authority with others. He allowed them to assist him in his work and in that process trained them for future responsibilities. When the time came, Joshua was ready to follow him in leadership. Joshua was not overwhelmed by the task because he was properly trained through mentoring and shepherding.

Moses's leadership qualities are important for all Christian leaders, whether they are professors or pastors. Although many individuals hold offices in ministry today, there is a shortage of good leaders. A political process will not create a leader like Moses; only a biblical model of leadership training will produce leaders who follow in the footsteps of Moses. (We will look at the ministry of empowered servant leadership in chapter 8.)

Ministry as Relationship

Ministry is a relational enterprise. One could say that God so loved the world that He initiated a relationship with the world through His Son, Jesus. Christians are called to stay in relationship with God and to invite others into such a relationship based on reconciliation. A minister's job is to plead with the world, "Be reconciled to God."

God made humankind in His own image. In the beginning, three harmonious relationships existed: between Adam and God, between Adam and Eve, and Adam with himself. Sin broke down all three relationships. Adam became afraid of God, began to blame Eve, and became ashamed of himself. Fear, blame, and shame became part of the dynamics of life for the first humans, and actually these tendencies have carried over into dysfunctional families today. Jesus Christ came into the world to reconcile these and other relationships that have been broken due to sin. Ministry is the vehicle through which this work is done; it is relational work.

Incarnational Presence

According to Saint Paul, a Christian's body is the temple of the Holy Spirit (1 Cor. 6:19); that is, the Holy Spirit dwells in a believer. Incarnational presence represents the idea that when a Christian minister is present with someone in need, he or she brings the presence of Christ with him or her in some unexplainable way. While ministry involves both being and doing, the concept of incarnational presence represents both being and doing at the same time. Being present fully with someone in the name of Jesus is a ministerial practice. This ministry has great potential especially when one is working with persons who are suffering and hurting. You may have noticed that people in pain do not remember a minister's words as much as his or her presence in the long run.

Incarnational presence is a way of communicating Christian hope. Paul's words in Colossians undergird this idea—"Christ in you is the hope of glory" (Col. 1:27). A minister practicing incarnational presence is living with the realization that just being with a suffering person can help bring about healing. Authentic Christian presence can be a healing experience. This ministry does not necessarily require the use of words.

One may conclude that Paul was seeking incarnational presence when he requested Timothy to "come before winter." His longing to be with members of various communities of faith as expressed in his letters (Rom. 1:11; Phil. 2:24) point out the value he placed on presence. In this day of virtual reality and cyber presence, ministers may want to consider the importance of this ministry of physical presence that was highlighted by Paul when writing on papyrus was the latest technology available.

Ministry as Memory

It appears that there is a legitimate ministry that can be called "remembering." In this age of great concern about the increasing number of people being afflicted with Alzheimer's disease (which profoundly affects memory), I consider this a sobering revelation.

The Bible speaks much about God and humankind in relation to memory and remembrance. God remembers His covenant (Ex. 6:5). He does not remember our forgiven sins (Isa. 43:25), but remembers righteous individuals—both men and women. Noah, Abraham, and Hannah are examples.

We are told not to forget God's dealings with us, but to remember them, and to pass on the memory to a new generation (Deut. 11:19). Israel was instructed not to forget that they were slaves in Egypt (Deut. 16:12), and to remember the Sabbath (Ex. 20:8). The psalmist instructs us not to forget "all His benefits" (Ps. 34:2).

Memory is at the heart of Christian theology. The undisputed instruction of Jesus on the night in which He was betrayed was to "do this in remembrance of me." The ordinances of even the most nontraditional faith groups are built on remembrance! Noticeably, theologian Henri Nouwen defined ministry as being a living reminder of Jesus.

Memory is a matter of great interest and special concern to Saint Paul. He tells us to remember Jesus (2 Tim. 2: 8). He instructs further: Remember the poor (Gal. 2:10); "Remember my chains" (Col. 4:18). The author of Hebrews adds: "Continue to remember those in prison as if you were together with them in prison, and those who are mistreated as if you yourselves were suffering" (Heb. 13:3). "Remember your leaders, who spoke the word of God to you" (Heb. 13:7).

In Paul's writings, the ministry of memory is strongly related to prayer. "We remember before our God and Father your work produced by faith ..." (1 Thess. 1:3). "I constantly remember you in my prayers" (2 Tim. 1: 3). "I thank my God every time I remember you" (Phil. 1:3). "I have not stopped giving thanks for you, remembering you in my prayers" (Eph. 1:16). "I always thank my God as I remember you in my prayers" (Phil. 1:4).

What a powerful ministry! Anyone with the ability to remember can do this ministry. There are no geographical limitations. Words may not even be needed for this ministry. Believers of all nations, tribes, and tongues can engage in this ministry of memory and remembrance, a ministry in which we connect our memory of one another to God.

The ministry of memory is not only about those who are living. Certainly, the leaders we are expected to remember according to Hebrews 13: 7 are not all alive. Some have finished their course and have gone to be with the Lord. They don't need our prayers, only our grateful memory.

As a person raised in a pastor's home in South India, I remember people outside my family who have touched my life in profound ways. Some of them are alive, others have finished their race. A Hindu woman who was forced to give up her eyes to follow Jesus is one of them. A retired teacher who found time to teach me English hymns, church members who shared their modest means with their pastor's kid, preachers who let me carry their Bibles, and classmates who left an imprint on my life. The list is long.

A young cancer patient I visited three decades ago is also on my list. I was a chaplain at the City of Faith Hospital in Tulsa, Oklahoma. The patient was a born-again Christian who had no family members to visit her. Her mother and grandmother had died from the same disease, her father was dead, and she had no siblings. She lived alone and kept her sickness a secret as long as she could due to fear. According to the doctors, the prognosis was not good because by the time she came to the hospital the disease had progressed significantly. One day she asked me during a pastoral visit, "I have no family left. I don't know how long I will live. Can I ask you for a favor?" Thinking that she would ask for some practical help, I said, "Of course, what can I do for you?" She asked, "Would you remember me once I am gone?" Moved by her unexpected request, I said, "Certainly. I will remember you." She thanked me.

I have seen many answers to prayers. I have witnessed both instant and gradual healings, but this was not the case with the young cancer patient. She passed away the following night.

There are times when all you can give others is your prayers and your memory! Sometimes God answers the prayers immediately. Other times, the answers come slowly. In some cases, the answer is not what one expects. In any case, we must pray, and we must remember.

Contemporary Images

According to Donald E. Messer, ministry today suffers from being perceived through stereotypical images.[12] He believes that many people consider ministers either hired hands or superhuman saints. These images distort the true meaning of ministry as a gift of God to all God's people. Several contemporary images of ministry are summarized below.

1. Minister as wounded healer in the community of the compassionate. In this view, the church is the compassionate community, and the minister brings healing to others as a wounded person on his or her own journey toward wholeness.
2. Minister as servant leader in a servant church. Here the church is a community of servants and ministers are servant-leaders.
3. Minister as political mystic in a prophetic community. This view sees the church as a community called to speak

prophetically to the world, and ministers are political mystics who do not conform to the world and its systems.
4. Minister as enslaved liberator of the rainbow church. The church in this view is a multicultural global community that stands for liberation of all people from all forms—social, political, economic, and so forth—of enslavement. Ministers are liberators who are themselves slaves (servants) of Christ.
5. Minister as practical theologian in a post-denominational church. The church here is not only nondenominational; it is a post-denominational community of faith. Ministers are practical theologians who empower lay leaders to do the work of the ministry.
6. Minister as good shepherd in a global village. The world has become a global village; the church is the flock of God. Ministers are shepherds who feed and lead the sheep.

According to William Willimon, contemporary images of ministry include the following:

1. Minister as media personality
2. Minister as political negotiator
3. Minister as therapist
4. Minister as manager
5. Minister as resident activist
6. Minister as preacher
7. Minister as servant leader[13]

Willimon proposes that ministry should be countercultural, since according to the scripture, ministers are aliens and exiles (1 Pet. 2:11). He believes that ministry must recover its classical forms of preaching, teaching, evangelizing, and healing as it responds to the critical needs of the church and the world.

Willimon sees ministry as an act of God and of the church. He believes that to be a pastor is to be intimately connected to the church; thus, ministry is a difficult vocation. Willimon defines ordination as an act of Christ and His church, for service to Christ and His church. According to him, ordination arises from above "as a gift of the Holy Spirit" (2 Tim. 1:6). It also arises from below, from the church's need for leadership. The process of ordination forms those who are to serve as priests for their position within a community of priests. It sets those apart who are to serve as examples. Ordination is an act of collegiality, made effective through the laying on of hands (1 Cor. 3:5-9).

Rewards of Ministry

Scripture compares ministry to work in a vineyard because it is hard labor. Ministry is not for those who seek ease and comfort, but for individuals who are committed to working toward greater rewards. The parable of the laborers in the vineyard illustrates the truth that God will reward all His faithful servants (Matt. 20:1-15). Some came to work early in the morning; others came at the third hour, the sixth hour, and the eleventh hour. The Master told them He would pay them whatever was right. When the evening came, each one received the same pay regardless of his starting time, and those who came earlier began to complain. The Master responded:

> Friend, I am not being unfair to you. Didn't you agree to work for a denarius? Take your pay and go. I want to give the man who was hired last the same as I gave you. Don't I have the right to do what I want with my own money? Or are you envious because I am generous? (Matt. 20:13-15)

Different interpretations of this passage exist, but one thing is very clear: A fair reward is promised to the faithful laborer. In fact, all laborers will be rewarded equally. Scholars have struggled to understand this passage, because from a worldly perspective the pay scale seems unfair. I agree with William Willimon that a more reflective reading of the parable provides the deeper interpretation that the pay is Jesus Himself. Jesus is the ultimate reward, and no greater currency could be given to any worker in God's vineyard. In other words, those who have Jesus have everything they need. "He who did not spare his own Son, but gave him up for us all—how will he not also, along with him, graciously give us all things?" (Rom. 8:32).

Chapter 2
Ministry: A Historical Perspective

Remember your leaders, who spoke the word of God to you.
Consider the outcome of their way of life and imitate their faith.
—Hebrews 13:7

A look at ministry from a historical perspective will help us to review the important elements of historic Christian ministry that should be of concern to all Christians. The premise of this chapter is that Spirit-filled ministry is not a new invention; it is not the product of twentieth-century Pentecostal revival. Christian ministry was expected to be empowered by the Holy Spirit from the very beginning (Acts 1:8). The disciples of Jesus were instructed not to make any move in ministry until they received the power of the Holy Spirit. They were asked by the ascending Christ to wait in Jerusalem until they received the power from above. Their waiting resulted in the events of the day of Pentecost and the ministry that followed.

General Story of Christianity

No one expected the small band of followers of a crucified Galilean to become the largest religious group in the world. It was natural for people to expect this sect to disband, as had similar groups led by Theudas, Judas, and the like (Acts 5:35-37), but God had other plans. The crucified Galilean was raised from the dead, and His followers took the message of His resurrection all over the world. Kings and kingdoms responded to that message, and ultimately nations and continents were transformed by it. Some understood the message of Jesus, while others misunderstood its implications. Some used it for their own advantage; others abused it. The history of the world is intricately connected with the story of Jesus, and the history of ministry is the story of its messengers.

The New Testament contains only a few decades of Christian history. The primary group of Christians in Jerusalem, the church led by James, the brother of Jesus, was scattered as a result of persecution. These Jewish Christians spread the good news of Christ all over the world, but it was the impact of the church in the margin at Antioch that spread the message among the Gentiles. Eventually, Rome became the center of Christian activities. As the number of Christians increased, so did the degree of persecution. The second and third centuries were periods of severe Christian persecution.

The next period was an era in which the Christian church battled the pervasive influence of heresies against the gospel message. Amazingly, many of those heresies are still in existence today, attempting to enter the mainstream of Christianity under different names and leaders. Many who refuse to study the history of the church keep repeating that history because they have not bothered to learn from past mistakes.

The Emperor Constantine's conversion and policies made Christianity a national religion. Yet, Christianity was not ready for such upward mobility. Suddenly, half the population of the Roman

Empire was Christian; their new status transformed Christianity from the religion of the persecuted to the religion of princes. The church as the kingdom of God seemed to match all other kingdoms in all possible ways! There was no longer a need to preach about the coming kingdom of God when such a powerful kingdom, with so many benefits, was already at hand. The church went through a serious period of backsliding. During this era, organizational authority became more important to the church leadership than spiritual power.

As church history continued, the world witnessed the formation and impact of doctrines, heresies, monasticism, scholasticism, an East-West split, and unbiblical crusades. These were followed by the emergence of the Reformation, missionary movements, Holiness revivals, awakenings, revivalists, separatists, the Pentecostal movement, Ecumenism, and other national and global Christian movements. All of these movements involved powerful personalities. Many settings became part of the Christian story: Jerusalem, Antioch, Rome, Constantinople, Worms, Wales, Topeka, and Azusa, just to name a few. The various movements and their respective locations significantly impacted both the understanding and the practice of Christian ministry.

A Brief History of Ministry

It is difficult to summarize the history of ministry, because any attempt to do so is inherently simplistic. One can state with confidence, however, that ministry in the apostolic age was Spirit-empowered. It emphasized preaching, teaching, and healing with the presence of signs, wonders, and miracles. Signs and wonders confirmed the preaching of the Word. Persecution of the ministers was almost guaranteed during this period. This was the pattern of ministry from Jerusalem to Patmos, spanning Acts to Revelation.

During the period of the church fathers, ministry generally was characterized by a form of godliness rather than by spiritual power. Although the church provided sound and helpful teaching, ministry in those days was sacramental and symbolic. The emphasis was no longer on preaching, teaching, and healing with accompanying signs, wonders, and miracles. Instead, the church established itself in codified doctrines and in the creation of hierarchies to manage the growing enterprise. Ministry became more reclusive during this period, characterized by monks and monasteries. The nature of ministry was contemplative, and thus it was predominately detached from the common people. Christian disciplines were developed during this time period, while clerical learning was emphasized.

The longer period, often called the Dark Ages, preceded the Protestant Reformation. *Sola scriptura,* "only scripture," was the slogan of the reformers, and preaching became the primary focus of ministry. Ministers during the time of the Reformation were preachers who recaptured the preaching aspect of ministry from the New Testament. The preaching of salvation through faith in Jesus Christ became the primary task of ministry. The revivals that followed this message greatly impacted ministry. For example, Methodism emphasized discipleship and lay ministries. The American awakenings produced preachers who emphasized conversion and holiness. Ministers were primarily concerned with saving souls during this period. Along with full-time pastors, evangelists, and revivalists, laypersons found ministry opportunities in many places.

The evangelical and Holiness revivals of the eighteenth and nineteenth centuries set the stage for the Pentecostal movement in the early twentieth century. Beginning like a river with multiple streams and eventually reaching throughout the world, the

Pentecostal movement produced ministers who believed in the present-day operation of the Holy Spirit. They began to preach, teach, baptize, and lead people to the rediscovered baptism in the Holy Spirit. They also rediscovered the gifts of the Holy Spirit and began to exercise those gifts in their ministries. The gift of speaking in tongues and the ministry of divine healing seemed to receive more attention than other operations of the Holy Spirit. Ministers were trained through mentoring and Bible institutes. They studied the Bible and learned practical ministries under the tutelage of experienced ministers.

The beginning of the modern Pentecostal movement witnessed ministry models that transcended color and gender. This period soon passed, as racially segregated, male-dominated Pentecostal denominations were formed. Pentecostals began to go out into the world as full gospel missionaries, following the example of major missionary enterprises of the previous centuries. Missionary pastors took the Pentecostal message far and near, doing the work of shepherding, evangelizing, and educating.

A new movement, called the Charismatic movement, began to emerge by the middle of the twentieth century. This complex movement impacted Catholics and Protestants alike. Oral Roberts, founder and chancellor of Oral Roberts University, and Demos Shakarian, pioneer of the Full Gospel Businessmen's Fellowship International, were two of the leaders of this emerging movement. The Charismatic movement produced lay ministers who, as part of their Christian walk, evangelized and led people to receive the baptism of the Holy Spirit. Ministry was not limited to ordained clergy or identified churches; for all practical purposes the Charismatics underscored the concept of the priesthood of all believers.

While the Pentecostals emphasized divine healing and the baptism in the Holy Spirit, with speaking in tongues as the initial physical evidence of Spirit baptism, the Charismatics gave priority to tongues as a prayer language, along with signs and wonders. Eventually, independent Charismatic churches and Word, faith, and prosperity ministries came out of the Charismatic movement. Often leaders of these ministries were not Bible college graduates, but believers who had experienced what they were teaching and had been mentored by independent ministers. Many of the churches within the Charismatic movement became megachurches, led by pastors who saw themselves as ranchers rather than shepherds. These churches utilized cell groups or other small group models to meet the spiritual needs of the majority of their members. Churches generally trained leaders for these small groups in basic ministry skills; many developed their own Bible institutes and ministry training centers to equip the large number of lay ministers they needed.

The end of the twentieth century witnessed new openness for formal training and continuing education in ministry on the part of the Pentecostals and Charismatics. Today, many working pastors attend Bible colleges and seminaries to retool themselves for ministry in these challenging times. Pentecostal and Charismatic institutions of learning are responding to the increasing educational needs of this growing movement.

A brief review of the history of ministry during the last two millennia leads one to make the following observations. One can make two mistakes in ministry and ministry preparation. The first mistake is to neglect the life and power of the Holy Spirit in ministry; this produces lifeless traditions and a stale church. On the other hand, it is also a major mistake to ignore the history of the church. Even those who are empowered by the Holy Spirit must learn the history of the Christian church, because ignorance of the past leads many to repeat the mistakes of the past. In other words, old heresies often show up as new teachings. People who have not studied their history take the risk of embracing such heresies as fresh revelations.

The Particular Story of Shepherding

The Old Testament describes the shepherding ministry of prophets and priests who were servants of the Shepherd-God. The New Testament presents Jesus Christ as the great Shepherd of the new covenant who gave up His life for the sheep. He appointed apostles, prophets, evangelists, pastors, and teachers to continue His work of perfecting the saints. Pastor-teachers are to lead (Acts 20:28–31), guide (1 Pet. 2:25), instruct (1 Tim. 2:7), and correct (2 Tim. 4:2) the people of God. They are also instructed to feed (John 21:15), edify (2 Cor. 13:10), build up (Eph. 4:12), comfort (2 Cor. 1:3–4), rebuke (Tit. 1:13), warn (Acts 20:31), and watch over souls (Heb. 13:17).

In *A Caring Church*, Charles Ver Straten sees the connection between the Old and New Testaments in the area of shepherding. He points out that Jesus, the good shepherd, *intentionally* trained His apostles to do the work of the ministry. Jesus ordained His disciples so that they could preach, teach, heal, and drive out demons (Matt. 9:36–38; Mk. 3:14, 15; 6:13), but New Testament ministry consisted of much more than action and performance; pastoral ministry in the New Testament was a ministry of the heart. According to Ver Straten, this ministry of the heart was demonstrated in the fundamental difference between the Jewish elders, who were basically administrators, and the Christian elders, *presbyteros*, who were primarily shepherds.[1]

Church Fathers on Pastoral Work

The second-century church apparently viewed the bishop as the successor to the apostle. While this was a deviation from the practice of the primitive church, it emphasizes the importance the early church gave to pastoral work and ministry. The pastoral concern of the early church is seen in Polycarp's description of the qualifications of a presbyter: "[They] must be compassionate, merciful towards all men, turning back the sheep that are gone astray, visiting all the infirm, not neglecting a widow or an orphan or a poor man."[2]

The writings of the church fathers provide clear evidence of the strong position of pastoral care in the ministry of the developing church. Both the person of the minister and the ministerial method received their attention. Thomas Oden did a great service by providing a collection of these writings in his series entitled *Classical Pastoral Care*.[3] Gregory the Great, for instance, advised pastors to be people who "out of affection of heart sympathize with another's infirmity." John Chrysostom emphasized the importance of training for pastoral ministry:

> Anyone who is about to enter upon this ministry needs to explore it all thoroughly beforehand and only then to undertake this ministry. And why? Because if he studies the difficulties beforehand he will at any rate have the advantage of not being taken by surprise when they crop up.[4]

The shepherding metaphor is strongly evident in the writings of early fathers. Origen writes, "The good Shepherd makes it His business to seek for the best pastures for His sheep, and to find green and shady groves where they may rest during the noonday heat."[5] Cyprian advises, "Therefore, dearly beloved Brother, take heed that the undisciplined be not consumed and perish, that you rule the brotherhood as far as possible with salutary counsels, and that you counsel each one for his salvation."[6] Chrysostom saw shepherding as an awesome responsibility. He made sure that the limits of the shepherding metaphor were not ignored:

> You cannot treat human beings with the same authority with which the shepherd treats a sheep. Here too it is possible to bind and to forbid food and to apply cautery and the knife, but the decision to receive treatment does not lie with the one who administers the medicine but actually with the patient.[7]

The need for preparation for pastoral work is seen in the writings of Origen and Tertullian. Origen compared priests studying secular subjects to the spoiling of the Egyptians by the Israelites when they left Egypt. Tertullian did appreciate the need for secular scholarship for polemic reasons, but he cautioned against uncritical reliance on secular knowledge for the work of the ministry. "What indeed has Athens to do with Jerusalem? What concord is there between the Academy and the Church? What between heretics and the Christians?" he asked.

Ministerial self-awareness and congruence were important to the early fathers. "You cannot put straight in others what is warped in yourself," said Athanasius. Black Moses, a third-century African ascetic, said, "If a man's deeds are not in harmony with his prayer, he labors in vain."

Pastoral ministry in the early church gave priority to the resources of the church, such as the Word, prayer, and sacraments. The Word of God was considered to be central to the care of souls. Pastoral prayer and the sacraments of baptism and communion also served as noble instruments of care.

Teaching was an important ministry in the early church, as church leaders assumed that through teaching the Word of God, one could guide souls toward higher levels of virtue. Clement of Alexandria and Athanasius wrote on the pedagogical aspects of ministry, considering Jesus as their model teacher. They noted that He also embodied His own teachings.

The community of faith continued to be an important resource in the care of souls. The church as the body of Christ served as the context for caregiving, but it also participated in that ministry. In addition to being the sacramental community of healing, the congregation became a provider of care by financially supporting the needy as well as the priestly caregivers.

Reconciliation was a major theme of ministerial work in the early church. Polycarp, Bishop of Smyrna, wrote about his approach to dealing with fallen clergy: "You have to restore them, like parts of your own person that are ailing and going wrong, so that the whole body can be maintained in health." The ministry of reconciliation also incorporated counseling as a major aspect of shepherding in the early church. Caregivers considered empathy to be a very important ingredient of good soul care.

Early writings conceptualized the counselor in the following capacities. The caregiver was a physician bringing healing to hurting people and a guide to those on a spiritual journey. He set people free from bondages and taught them like a faithful educator.

The church fathers wrote about the methodological issues of pastoral counseling, which are still relevant today. They paid attention to the importance of silence, the use of language, and the reading of body language. For them, counseling was not value-neutral; pastors were expected to give moral counseling. The scripture provided them with moral guidance. These writers also emphasized the importance of using one's words wisely, paying particular attention to the use of language in counseling and ministry. The work of the ministry required spiritual discernment, which meant that caregivers had to be open to the Spirit and the Word to exercise appropriate wisdom in their work. Scriptural counsel had to be given with spiritual discernment.

According to Thomas Oden, the artificial separation of psychology, ethics, and theology did not exist in classical pastoral care. The early church acknowledged the tension between guilt and forgiveness, grace and effort, discipline and freedom, and law and gospel. They maintained a balance between the sternness of the law and the mercy of the gospel.

Crisis ministries were also part of classical pastoral work. Many classical writers discussed the importance and methodologies of crisis intervention, with special emphasis on the care of the sick. The church made a particular effort to offer the ministries of the church to the seriously sick and dying. Early pastoral writers discussed the subject of suffering in detail, as pastoral work required an honest encounter with this issue. These writers struggled with the issue of theodicy. The connection between evil and suffering was of considerable interest to them. They gave careful attention to the care of the poor and widowed, providing special instructions regarding the obligations of the church to the poor and needy. The care of the poor involved more than just offering pastoral support; it also included the offering of food, drink, shelter, and clothing.

Classical pastoral writers did not neglect the process and meaning of death in their writing. They explained how to prepare people for dying, and how to minister to those who are left behind. Christian hope is at the center of such ministry.

Pastoral Care during the Middle Ages and Pre-Reformation Period

Although the Charismatic tradition was often seen as part of various heresies throughout history, Eddie Hyatt has traced the history of the church through the Dark Ages to show that a Charismatic tradition survived in spite of suppression and persecution.[8]

Although the church of the Middle Ages became corrupt in many ways, the ministry of pastoral care flourished during this period in the form of spiritual direction, especially in the monastic tradition. A more biblical and classical model of pastoral care took place among the Cathari (ca. 1050), Albigenses (ca. 1140), and Waldenses (ca. 1173) The theological positions held by pre-Reformation reformers like John Wycliffe (1324–1384), John Huss (1373–1415), and William Tyndale (1494–1536) played an important role in keeping ministry biblical as opposed to papal.

The Reformers and Pastoral Ministry

The Reformation brought the primacy of the Word of God back to Christian ministry. Preaching the Word became the priority of the minister, but pastoral care was also a major concern. Martin Luther, John Calvin, and Ulrich Zwingli particularly emphasized the importance of the pastoral task of caregiving. Luther wrote about the importance of soul care and of the preparation required of ministers who desired to do it:

> Therefore I admonish you, especially those of you who are to become instructors of consciences, as well as each of you individually, that you exercise yourselves by study, by reading, by meditation, and by prayer, so that in temptation you will be able to instruct consciences, both your own and others', console them, and take them from the Law to grace, from active righteousness to passive righteousness, in short, from Moses to Christ.[9]

Although Luther believed in the priesthood of all believers, he held the pastoral office at a more distinctive level. He considered the scriptures to be the best textbook for pastors. Concerning the writings of the fathers, Luther said:

> We are like men who study the sign-posts and never travel the road. The dear fathers wished, by their writings, to lead us to the Scriptures, but we so use them as to be led away from the Scriptures, though the Scriptures alone are our vineyard in which we ought all to work and toil.[10]

Luther, "put great emphasis on pastoral care, which always related directly to the ministry of the Word."[11] Luther believed in an incarnational approach to pastoral ministry. "When Christ wished to attract and instruct men," Luther said, "He had to become a man. If we are to attract and instruct children, we must become children with them."[12] Luther also believed in unconditional love as a requirement for helping relationships. He believed that "there is no person on earth so bad that he does not have something about him that is praiseworthy."[13] For Luther, pastoral work involved much more than preaching and teaching; it involved nurturing.

> Therefore, something more than merely preaching the Law is required, that a man may also know how he may

be enabled to keep it. Otherwise what good does it do to preach that Moses and the Law merely say: This thou shalt do; this God requires of thee. Yes, my dear Moses, I hear what you say; and it is no doubt right and true. But do tell me where am I to get the ability to do what I have unfortunately not done and cannot do.[14]

Soul care must involve enabling people to live the Christian life in a practical way. Anyone can share with others what they ought to be doing, but it takes a caring pastor to help people live a virtuous life.

Luther understood the importance of having a theology of suffering; his own theology was built on Christian hope. He believed that "whatever hurts and distresses us does not happen to hurt or harm us but is for our good and profit. We must compare this to the work of the vinedresser who hoes and cultivates his vine."[15]

Calvin believed that the ministry of a pastor involved proclaiming the Word, instructing, admonishing, exhorting privately and publicly, censuring, and enjoining "brotherly corrections." Obviously, pastoral care and counseling were important aspects of ministry as Calvin envisioned it. He believed that the pastor must do preaching, governing, and pastoring. "A pastor needs two voices," he said, "one for gathering the sheep and the other for driving away wolves and thieves. The Scripture supplies him with the means for doing both."[16] Calvin saw the ministry of caring as an aspect of the ministry of *diakonia* or service. The thrust of this ministry involved caring for the poor and the sick.

Martin Bucer (1491–1551) was a disciple of Luther and a teacher of Calvin. According to Switzinger, he identified four duties of the pastor: (1) teach Holy Scriptures, (2) administer sacraments, (3) participate in the discipline of the church, and (4) care for the needy.

Pastoral Work during Post-Reformation Period

The concept of ministry that the reformers envisioned continued in the post-Reformation Church. Puritan pastors, for instance, were to be preachers and caregivers. They were expected to live a godly life and deliver the message of reconciliation to humanity. Puritans saw the minister as a double interpreter, interpreting God to humankind and interpreting humankind to God.

Winthrop S. Hudson described the state of the ministry during the Puritan era. While preaching was considered the most important pastoral act, pastoral care was considered essential. The pastoral duties of ministers were well defined: "These were the major facets of the minister's pastoral duties—catechizing, visiting, disciplining, and counseling the members of his flock."[17] Visitation was seen as a very important pastoral duty, so that people would be prepared for a "fruitful life or a happy death." In fact, the pastoral visit was "regarded as a doubly important adjunct because the proper ordering of family life was a major disciplinary concern."[18]

Pastoral counseling was also of great concern to the Puritan pastor. According to Hudson, "Pastoral counseling was everywhere regarded as one of the most important as well as the most difficult of the pastoral duties."[19] Clergy were highly encouraged to qualify themselves to be good counselors, because it was well recognized that unskilled counselors could aggravate the "griefs and perplexities" people experienced. Many manuals were produced to help pastors deal with difficult cases. Situations involving moral perplexities in relation to family life, economic activities, political issues, and employment-related problems were common.

Jonathan Edwards (1703–1758) and other famous pastors of the eighteenth century saw themselves as people charged with the proclamation of the gospel and the care of the saints' souls. Ministry involved honoring God and saving humankind, and saving humankind involved serving them in the name of Christ.

John Wesley (1703–1791) was concerned about the salvation, spiritual growth, and nurture of individuals. He is associated with the doctrine of Christian perfection. William Salsbery states that the ministry of pastoral care experienced a renewal under Wesley's ministry, as it "was structured within a biblical framework."[20] In this framework, he found a rationale for developing lay shepherds. Wesley conceptualized a lay preacher/pastor as a gifted person called by God to be trained and sent. The lay leaders taught and cared for their classes, but each leader was under the supervision of Wesley. The lay pastor was expected to see each person in the class once a week and meet with the minister and the stewards of the society once a week.

The nineteenth century provided a good number of faithful ministers. Charles Spurgeon (1834–1892), although he was mostly known for his preaching, was a great pastor. He had a clear understanding of the purpose of ministry. Other great nineteenth-century pastors include Charles Bridges (1794–1869) and G. Campbell Morgan (1863–1945). The modern Pentecostal movement was not born in a theological vacuum. Pentecostal ministry had good models to follow, even though it initially rebounded from them.

Ministry in America

The American national story is closely connected with matters of Christian faith and ministry. While one may argue about the religious orthodoxy of some of the nation's founding fathers, there is no way to separate faith and ministry from the life and adventures of the early settlers who arrived in the new land seeking freedom of religion and worship. Clergy played important roles in families and communities from the earliest days of the nation. They were involved in war and peace in the new land. American life has always been marked by puritan holiness and a protestant work ethic.

The Evangelicals

Sydney Mead focuses on the history of pastoral ministry in America, stating that the concept of ministry among the American evangelicals underwent considerable change during the early history of Protestantism (1607–1850) in America. Perhaps the greatest change was the loss of the priestly function of ministry. "It is obvious that within this broad context the conception of the minister practically lost its priestly dimension as traditionally conceived and became that of a consecrated functionary, called of God, who directed the purposive activities of the visible church."[21] Ministers primarily worked at the conversion of souls; the work of a minister was judged essentially by his success in this area and the pastor's caregiving and nurturing skills became secondary. According to Mead, "When pietistic sentiments and revivalist techniques swept to the crest of evangelicalism in America, the conversion of souls tended to crowd out other aspects of ministers' work."[22]

The second half of the nineteenth century turned out to be a time of significant positive change for American ministry. Faced with industrialization, urbanization, and the challenges of atheism and Darwinism, the church had to pay special attention to the spiritual needs of people. Although the preaching of the Word still took priority, Christian education and pastoral care also received considerable attention during this period (1850–1950). According to Robert Michaelsen:

Protestant ministers have carried on a quietly effective work over the years as pastors, as comforters of the sick, the distressed and the bereaved, as counselors of the perplexed, as guides and guardians to those seeking spiritual light and moral rectitude. But we have seen in the last half-century (1900–1950) an increasing awareness of the importance of the minister as pastor.[23]

Seminary curriculum began to particularly emphasize systematic training in pastoral care during this period. The clinical training movement was born as a reaction to traditional theological training, which was not preparing ministers to deal with the personalities and struggles of people.

Pentecostal-Charismatic Ministry

The dawn of the twentieth century witnessed the birth of the modern Pentecostal movement. Tracing its American roots to a Bible college in Topeka, Kansas, this movement spread to Houston, to Azusa Street in Los Angeles, and eventually to the entire world. (Some segments of modern Pentecostal movements, such as the 1905 revival at Mukti Mission of Pandita Ramabai in India, cannot be directly connected to Topeka.) The spread of Pentecostalism had an impact on Protestant ministry, as Pentecostals began to emphasize speaking in tongues and divine healing in their churches. They also emphasized evangelism and leading people to the baptism of the Holy Spirit. Pentecostal pastors became involved in the ministry of divine healing.

In spite of their interest in divine healing, the Pentecostals were also more concerned about the saving of souls than the care of souls. Early classical Pentecostals, followed by Charismatics and the subsequent neo-charismatics called third-wavers, kept the same emphasis. While divine healing was a theological characteristic of the Pentecostals, the denominational and independent Charismatics emphasized healing as a major ministry theme. Although healing was a pastoral theme among all Spirit-filled believers, the method of ministry used was often evangelistic rather than pastoral.

It would appear that three unique circumstances initially kept Pentecostals from developing in the area of pastoral care. First, the Charismatic aspect of their worship meant that ministry often took place in the sanctuary. The Holy Spirit did the ministry, so the pastors' skills in this area were not a matter of great concern. The second issue was the puritanical holiness to which most Pentecostals were committed. This meant that many issues requiring pastoral care were seen instead as disciplinary issues. Concern for the individual experiencing the emotional aftermath of divorce, for example, was less important than the issue of disciplining the divorced person and preventing more divorces from occurring. For Pentecostals, caregiving was not the priority in such a situation. Third, Pentecostals were committed to eschatological evangelism. This position encouraged evangelism at all costs, on all occasions. A funeral was not simply a place to minister to the grieving and bereaved; a major objective was to utilize the funeral as an opportunity to win the lost souls who would be attending the service. Pentecostals were acutely aware that Jesus might come at any time, and they did not want to leave anyone unsaved.

Pastoral ministry among Charismatics varied among different groups of Charismatic believers. Mainline pastors who were Charismatic were generally trained in pastoral ministry, whereas independent Charismatics typically preferred the evangelistic healing approach. Megachurches within the Spirit-empowered movement were focused on sanctuary ministry involving public gathering and celebration. Unfortunately, the current trend is not much different in terms of Christian education and pastoral care.

A Thematic History

Charles Clebsch and William Jaekle, in their classic work *Pastoral Care in Historical Perspective*,[24] offer a thematic history of pastoral ministry. They found that certain theological themes relating to pastoral care dominated particular historical periods. These themes express the thrust of ministry during these periods.

Sustaining was the pastoral care theme in the early church. The apostles shared the Word, the deacons served the tables, and the practitioners of ministry were acknowledged as gifted people during this period.

The post-apostolic era embodied the theme of *reconciliation*. Pastoral care primarily involved reconciling troubled persons to God. The functional role of the pastor emerged during this period, when ministers began to receive pay for their services.

The theme of the fourth-century church, according to Clebsch and Jaekle, was *guidance*. Pastoral care then involved helping people live in accordance with well-defined Christian culture. The pastoral caregiver was to guide people out of secularism and non-Christian activities into Christian activities. Guidance continued to be the theme of pastoral care during the Dark Ages (AD 500–1400). However, as monasticism increased, the monks became interpreters of life. They identified seven deadly sins and defined a twelve-step ladder of humility.

Healing became the theme of pastoral care for medieval Christianity (1400–1550). A sacramental system was developed to address the maladies of life, including a sophisticated sacramental system of symbols: Its goal was to restore spiritual and physical health. There was much concern about the activities of demons, as caregivers wanted to provide power for living the Christian life.

Post-Reformation pastoral care (1550–1700) once again embraced the theme of *reconciliation*. Individuals needed reconciliation with God as well as internal and external disciplines to live righteous lives. The pastor was able to offer confessional forgiveness, but the church believed that pastors required special training.

During the Enlightenment (1700–1850) the church shifted its focus of care to *sustaining* and preserving faith. John Bunyan's *Pilgrim's Progress* was written during this period.

As evangelism and discipleship became the important issues of the missionary era (1850–1907), *guiding* and *healing* emerged as the themes of pastoral care. The establishment of hospitals and the YMCA, as well as the birth of the Salvation Army, became expressions of this emphasis. The themes of *reconciling* and *sustaining* once again predominated during the Revival period (1908–1919), as World War I caused great need in the Western population.

The next period (1920–1945), which witnessed the Japanese occupation and World War II, initiated a time of *healing* and *sustaining*. Nationalism was incorporated into the ministry, while the emphasis of the church became eschatological. During this time, the church needed to be concerned about its own survival.

Clebsch and Jaekle consider the period during the Korean War, between 1945 and 1953, the dark age of the modern church. As a result of the war, pastoral care focused on *sustaining* the church, and the following period was a time of rebuilding the church, with an emphasis on *guiding*. During the 1960s, the church continued its ministry of *sustaining* and *guiding*, while the seventies became a period of mass evangelism and a theme of *reconciliation*.

Clebsch and Jaekle describe *healing* as the main goal of pastoral care. They consider Christian education and preservation of traditions as defining the ministry of *sustaining*, whereas *guiding* involved devotional life, spiritual direction, leadership training, and discipleship. According to these authors, *reconciliation* dealt with evangelism and the issues of social structure.

Generally speaking, one can make a case for the continuing rotation of these themes as emphases in the ministry of the church from the last quarter of the twentieth century until now. However, due to the increased concern about whole person health and ecology, Howard Clinebell has suggested *nurturing* as a fifth emphasis during this period.[25] It will be interesting to watch the impact of this added theme in the years ahead.

Pastoral care practices in general have become less clinical in the new century. The postmodern culture is less interested in pastoral care models involving diagnosis and treatment. A narrative model of caregiving is becoming more dominant as caregivers consider more intentionally the larger sociocultural contexts of persons needing pastoral care and counseling. Carrie Doehring,[26] Karen D. Scheib,[27] and Deborah van Deusen Hunsinger[28] have written extensively on this approach to pastoral care.

Impact of Dominant Social Characters

It has been pointed out that ministry in America has often adopted models that are based on dominant contemporary social characters.[29] For instance, during the seventeenth and eighteenth centuries the educated *master* was the dominant social character; consequently, ministry adopted this model for itself. The master was an authoritative teacher who had something to say. He was a person formed by learning, and his authority was based on literature and learning. As a learned person, the master was expected to give intellectual leadership. He was considered holy due to his study of text.

In the nineteenth century, social change in the United States involved issues of pluralism and church-state relationships. At this time a different type of leadership was needed; society replaced the character of master with that of *orator*, so that oration replaced teaching. The church adopted this social model in turn, and produced "princes of the pulpit." The dominant ministry model became revivalist or pulpiteer. These individuals preached, thousands flocked to hear them as a form of dramatic or philosophical entertainment, and sinners were saved. They also founded congregations and built buildings to accommodate the growing churches. Regional groups were organized to manage the increased membership, and they devised plans to educate the masses of new church members.

The late nineteenth century and early twentieth century marked an increase in America's belief in science and technology. During this time the concept of profession emerged, and was adopted first by the fields of engineering and medicine. *Professionals* applied theory to solve problems. The church also adopted the professional model of ministry, and the minister became a builder, organizer, and motivator. Subsequently, ministers began to receive professional training in university settings.

The mission of the church became unclear in the 1930s and 1940s. According to Niebuhr, there was no single model of ministry during this period.[30] General optimism predominated regarding ecumenical theology. The minister functioned as pastoral *director* during this period. The pastoral director was similar but not identical to the builder. The builder built for the people brought in by the revivalist, while the director maintained institutions already built by others. The roles of preacher, teacher, and priest diminished, while the roles of manager and counselor increased. During the 1960s, the dominant social character was the *manager/ therapist*; as a result, the church adopted the manager/therapist model of ministry. The 1960s also marked a period of confusion about the theological foundations of ministry. What the manager did for the organization, namely solving internal problems, the therapist did for the individual. The minister functioned as organizational problem solver (therapist) as well as counselor of church members.

I attended Yale Divinity School during the 1970s. During that period, counseling and clinical pastoral education were the major emphases in theological education.

No one has yet defined the dominant social characters of the late twentieth century and the early twenty-first century. In retrospect, this was a period of major development in technology, multimedia, and communications. One could assert that *media personalities and corporate executives* were the dominant social characters during this period. Similarly, one could argue that ministry adopted these models. The popularity of megachurch ministries, as well as television and multimedia ministries, supports this perspective.

The preceding review of the changing dominant social figures demonstrates that the church was often influenced more by society than by its own biblical declarations. Although these adaptations were not necessarily wrong, they demonstrate that the church has often been more easily influenced by current culture than by God's Word. It is hoped that ministry in the future will be influenced more by the directives of the scripture than by the newly emerging dominant social characters.

Positive Ministry Trends in the New Century

I will conclude this section on a positive note by listing some of the trends I am seeing in healthy congregations across the country. These have developed because pastors have taken their contextual challenges seriously and decided to respond in thoughtful, prayerful, and reflective ways. Casting a positive vision, these leaders have mobilized their congregations to change and impact their communities.

1. Attempting to exegete the Word and the world and connect them, churches are targeting the specific needs of their communities with positive solutions.
2. Churches are developing and empowering lay leadership, reducing hierarchy, and accepting short-term commitments to serve.
3. Relationship building is emphasized through small groups with well-trained group leaders.
4. Pastors are strategically developing mission-driven churches by cultivating purpose-driven individuals.
5. Churches are exploiting technology and utilizing multimedia in new and creative ways.
6. Pastors and staff members are retooling themselves through educational experiences, leadership development, and self-care.
7. Churches are balancing seeker-friendly public worship with transformational discipleship programs.
8. Denominational churches are embracing a nondenominational approach to life in the community.

9. Churches are owning their present without disowning their past.
10. Churches are embracing the Holy Spirit without appearing unusual.
11. Churches are developing need-based programming and discontinuing truly expired traditional programs.
12. Pastors are seeking better understanding of their calling and assessing their ministries.

I hope these trends will continue and produce more effective and healthier congregations and many grateful pastors.

Chapter 3
Ministry and the Holy Spirit

> Be filled with the Spirit, speaking to one another
> with psalms, hymns, and songs from the Spirit.
> —Ephesians 5:18–19

Christian ministry is more than just a helping profession; it is the incarnational outcome of consecrated lives represented by life-giving service and living sacrifices of men and women who are called by God for His eternal purposes. The most important aspect of ministry is the minister's ongoing relationship with the One who called him or her. According to Mark, Jesus ordained the twelve that they might be with Him (Mark 3:14). They were to preach, teach, and bring deliverance to people, but being *with* Jesus was the priority, as it strengthened the relationship between the One who called and the ones called.

Moses's encounter with God at Mount Horeb gives us a clue to the mystery of God's call to service. Moses said to God, "Suppose I go to the Israelites and say to them, 'The God of your fathers has sent me to you,' and they ask me, 'What is his name?' Then what shall I tell them?" God said to Moses, "I AM WHO I AM. This is what you are to say to the Israelites: 'I AM has sent me to you'" (Ex. 3:13–14). God defines Himself as I AM, not I DO. Just as God's work in His universe flows out of His being, a minister's work must flow out of his or her being. A minister's being is more important than his or her doing; his or her identity at the core of his or her being must be anchored in God and His call.

It appears that ministers are always in the process of becoming. Jesus told His disciples that He would make them fishers of men. Christ's disciples were in the process of being made, and the making was to happen as they followed Him. God, through His Spirit, is molding His children and shaping them; He is working on making His children what they should become. In other words, He is working on His children's "being." The prophet Jeremiah writes about the potter's house and describes how the potter creates a vessel. That creative process is stressful for the vessel, but in order to become a vessel of honor, it must be willing to go through the challenging process. God does the molding and shaping of His people through His Spirit. Authentic Christian ministry is Spirit-filled, Spirit-led, and Spirit-empowered service; it is God's work done by God's servants who have been and are being molded by His hand.

In spite of all his or her preparation and training, a minister is completely dependent on the Holy Spirit. Ministry does not belong to the minister; it belongs to Christ. Human skills and resources are necessary, but they are not sufficient. I think of the words of Dean Collin Williams of Yale Divinity School, who said that the accumulation of all training in ministry equals no more than five loaves of bread. Until those loaves are given to the Master who will bless them, break them, and multiply them, the disciples cannot feed the multitude. Although ministers may have personal and religious resources at their disposal, ultimately the enabling of

God's Spirit makes the difference in their effectiveness. The power of the Spirit is the true dynamic in ministry. "You shall receive power when the Holy Spirit has come upon you" (Acts 1:8 NKJV). Authentic ministry is Spirit-empowered service in the name of Jesus. A ministry without the presence and power of the Holy Spirit is ineffective. The apostle Paul exhorted believers, "Be filled with the Spirit" (Eph. 5:18). He knew that by being filled with the Spirit, a believer would have access to the gifts of the Spirit and the opportunity to be formed by the fruits of the Spirit. Effective ministry requires both spiritual empowerment and character formation. True ministerial formation is a *spiritual* process of transformation.

When the Spirit Came

The key to understanding empowerment in ministry is to understand the impact of Pentecost on the disciples of Jesus. They were under instruction to wait for the coming of the Holy Spirit. They knew that the Spirit would empower them for service, but it is unclear if they knew what that would look like. The book of Acts presents a detailed narrative of their work following Pentecost, which is our clue to this dimension of life and service.

It appears that Pentecost introduced four unique spiritual characteristics that were incorporated into the apostles' ministry. These characteristics went beyond the summary description of post-Pentecostal life in Acts 2:42–47:

> They devoted themselves to the apostles' teaching and to fellowship, to the breaking of bread and to prayer. Everyone was filled with awe at the many wonders and signs performed by the apostles. All the believers were together and had everything in common. They sold property and

possessions to give to anyone who had need. Every day they continued to meet together in the temple courts. They broke bread in their homes and ate together with glad and sincere hearts, praising God and enjoying the favor of all the people. And the Lord added to their number daily those who were being saved.

Let us look at these characteristics briefly here.

1. The Holy Spirit Empowered Ministers

The ministry that followed the day of Pentecost was empowered. Human agents were involved and human efforts were needed, but what made the difference in the outcome of their work was divine presence and mediation. The Holy Spirit manifested as the source of power to witnesses beyond the disciples' abilities. They were empowered to minister healing (Acts 3:8). A new boldness possessed this petrified group (Acts 4:20; 5:29; 7:54-60; 9:31). Signs and wonders took place beyond the ministries of the apostles (Acts 8:8) in places far away from Jerusalem, the center of spiritual gravity. The Spirit began to move in the margins in places like Antioch through persons who were not the recognized administrators of the divine work.

2. The Holy Spirit Expanded the Vision

When the Spirit came, Christian ministry moved from being local to global. The disciples experienced an expansion of their vision. It seems that things Jesus had told them began to make more sense to them. They watched the 120 in the upper room becoming 3,000 in one day. The community grew, and their vision and mission expanded. The whole world was in Jerusalem on the day of Pentecost and Jerusalem was challenged to go to the whole world. The church was adding members at the beginning, but soon it seemed to be multiplying membership.

3. The Holy Spirit Embraced Diversity

The Spirit brought strangers into the church, and the church was able to embrace them. This was not always the case with the disciples. The Spirit began to remove internal and external hindrances to grow the church. Distance was no longer a barrier; Samaria and Antioch were reached. Gender was not a barrier to ministry; women were included in ministry. Sons and daughters were prophesying, finally (Acts 18:26; 21:9). Titles were not a barrier to ministry; deacons, not just apostles, were ministering signs and wonders. Race was not a barrier. The group of 120 in the upper room was basically a Jewish gathering, but in chapter 3, a handicapped person was coming in. In chapter 6, Greek women were being taken care of. Samaritans were coming in chapter 8. The Ethiopian, an African, came in chapter 10. The Gentile Cornelius was in by chapter 10. Lydia, the European woman, was in by chapter 16. The Spirit enabled the local group, mostly villagers, to embrace global diversity.

4. The Holy Spirit Transformed Individuals and Communities

The Holy Spirit transformed individuals and communities in the first empowered church. Communities were transformed in Jerusalem and Ephesus as everyone touched by the Spirit was personally transformed. Peter is the best case in point. Here is the disciple who said no to several key initiatives. He had said no to crucifixion. He was on record against Jesus washing his feet. He definitely said no to the idea of going to the house of a Gentile like Cornelius. He was, however, persuaded by unbelievable divine appointments to go and visit Cornelius. He preached Jesus at the house of this Gentile, and the results completely surprised him and everyone else involved.

While Peter was still speaking these words, the Holy Spirit came on all who heard the message. The circumcised believers who had come with Peter were astonished that the gift of the Holy Spirit had been poured out even on Gentiles. For they heard them speaking in tongues and praising God. Then Peter said, "Surely no one can stand in the way of their being baptized with water. They have received the Holy Spirit just as we have." (Acts 10:44-47)

Peter was never the same again. His transformation was complete, significant, and strategic for the purposes of God. Later, this very apostle who was adamant about having Judaic prerequirements for Christian initiation defended the opposite position on diversity at the Jerusalem conference (Acts 15:6-10). Amazing, indeed! The wind blows where it pleases. The fire burns as it pleases. The river flows in the desert. The Spirit transforms.

These characteristics manifested in the actual ministry practices of the early church. As a case can be made that ministry in Acts must be a prototype for Spirit-empowered ministry in all ages, it will be helpful to examine the themes and emphases of ministry practices in their earliest New Testament forms. What are the major elements of Spirit-empowered ministry one can discern in the earliest chapter of church history?

Ministry Practices in Acts

Ministry in the New Testament period clearly emphasized preaching, teaching, and healing, as well as signs, wonders, and miracles. A closer examination of the book of Acts provides a more detailed understanding of Spirit-empowered ministry practices which enabled the apostles to become witnesses from Jerusalem "to the ends of the earth."

One can discern five major themes that represent the thrust of Spirit-filled ministry in Acts: (1) prayer as ministry; (2) signs, wonders, and sacraments; (3) response to persecution; (4) praise and worship; and (5) enhancing fellowship. The following is an overview of these themes.

1. Ministry of Prayer

Prayer is a major theme of the book of Acts. The disciples pray in one place (Acts 1:14) and in one accord (Acts 2:1). Prayer is offered at the ordination of deacons (Acts 6:6), and Peter and John pray for the Samaritans to receive the baptism of the Holy Spirit (Acts 8:14, 15). Saul prays and learns that Ananias is on his way to minister to him (Acts 9:11, 12); Peter prays on a roof top and has a vision about God's plans for the Gentiles (Acts 10:9). The church prays for Peter during his imprisonment, and God answers the prayer (Acts 12:12). Similarly, Paul and Silas pray together in prison, and the prison doors open for them (Acts 16:25). The elders fast and pray on behalf of Paul and Barnabas in preparation for their ordination (Acts 13:2, 3), and Paul, on his way to prayer, meets Lydia, who receives the gospel (Acts 16:13, 14).

Spirit-filled ministry is a prayerful ministry; prayer must always be a part of ministry. The earliest church was involved in "the apostle's doctrines, fellowship, breaking of bread, and prayer" (Acts 2:42). Scripture strongly reinforces this emphasis, indicating that the apostles *devoted* themselves to "prayer and the ministry of the Word" (Acts 6:4). One can feel the human emotion of Ananias through his prayer, as he was instructed to visit the recent convert Saul: "Lord, I have heard many reports about this man" (Acts 9:13). A minister is compelled to pray about everything. This type of unceasing prayer moves beyond the realm of formal prayer and is expressed as the cry of one's heart raised toward heaven on behalf of someone or some situation. In prayer, one seeks God's will and His Word for any given situation. A prayer may turn out to be a groan.

2. Signs, Wonders, and Sacraments

Power-filled evangelism is another theme of the book of Acts. Essentially, Acts represents an empowered community engaged in power-filled ministry. This community baptized converts and broke bread from house to house. Supernatural manifestations of God's power were considered normative. The power of the Holy Spirit came (Acts 2:4), and shortly thereafter a lame man entered the temple walking, leaping, and praising God after he was healed (Acts 3:6-8). Ananias and Sapphira lied to the Holy Spirit and encountered death (Acts 5:3-5). Prison doors opened for the apostles by the power of God (Acts 5:17-19), and signs and wonders manifested in Samaria following the preaching of the gospel (Acts 8:5-8). Philip, the evangelist, was transported by the power of the Spirit (Acts 8:39); Peter walked out of the prison to join the assembled believers (Acts 12:7-11); and prison doors opened for Paul and Silas (Acts 16:26). The woman with an evil spirit was delivered by the power of God (Acts 16:18), and the Gentile, Cornelius, and his household received the power of the Holy Spirit just like the Jews in Jerusalem (Acts 10:44-46).

The power experienced by the community of believers in the book of Acts was multifaceted. They had the power of the apostles' teaching and the power of the Holy Spirit; yet they also enjoyed the power that came from holy living and a lifestyle of giving and receiving. Thus, the community was not only an empowered community, but also a love-filled community. Power and love were balanced in Acts so that ministry was more than the demonstration of power; it also included the impartation of divine love.

3. Pastoral Responses to Persecution

Ministry in the book of Acts evoked persecution, and the disciples' response to that persecution became a part of their ministry. Peter was threatened (Acts 4:18-21), imprisoned (Acts 5:17, 18), and beaten (Acts 5:40, 41). Stephen was stoned, but before the first stone hit his body, he looked up to heaven and saw the face of Jesus (Acts 7:55-60). Peter was imprisoned after James was killed (Acts 12:1-3), while unbelievers plotted to abuse Paul and Barnabas (Acts 14:5). Later, Paul and Silas were beaten and imprisoned (Acts 16:22, 23).

Scripture describes the apostles' response to their persecution, which became an encouragement for persecuted believers throughout history. Peter rejoiced for the privilege of suffering for the sake of the gospel (Acts 5:41), and Stephen's martyrdom impacted Saul of Tarsus (Acts 7:58, 8:1). After the church prayed in response to Peter's imprisonment and an angel released him, he became a living witness of the power of God. In the midst of their distressing circumstances, Paul and Silas ministered to the bewildered jailer and the confused prisoners who were caught in the miracle of the open prison (Acts 16:25-34). In the book of Acts, persecution is an outcome of ministry as well as a vehicle for ministry.

4. Praise and Worship

Ministry in the book of Acts consistently includes praise and worship of God. The disciples gathered to pray and praise God in the upper room (Acts 2:1-4, 11, 47), and the persecuted apostles praised God for the privilege of suffering (Acts 5:41). The healed lame man responded by walking, leaping, and praising God (Acts 3:8). The Ethiopian eunuch rejoiced in his salvation (Acts 8:39), and the household of Cornelius praised God as the Spirit gave them utterance (Acts 10:44–46). During the imprisonment of Paul and Silas, the praises of God filled the prison, which no longer could contain God's presence or His servants (Acts 16:25, 26).

5. Fellowship

Christian fellowship (*koinonia*) is a key element of ministry in the book of Acts, and facilitating fellowship is a pastoral responsibility. Scripture describes the disciples as being together in one accord, in one place.

> They devoted themselves to the apostles' teaching and to the fellowship, to the breaking of bread and to prayer … All the believers were together and had everything in common … Every day they continued to meet together in the temple courts. They broke bread in their homes and ate together with glad and sincere hearts, praising God and enjoying the favor of all the people. (Acts 2:42, 44–47)

It is clear that the earliest Christians believed in fellowship. They shared their lives with one another, worshiped together, and suffered together. In the midst of persecution and challenges, they practiced Christian presence and fellowship.

Understanding Empowerment

Spirit-filled ministry is an empowered ministry. One cannot obtain kingdom outcomes with one's own personal power; God's work requires God's power. Even the Son of God relied on the power of the Spirit. "The Spirit of the Lord is upon me," Jesus said (Luke 4:18). He also instructed His disciples to wait in Jerusalem until they received power from heaven. "But you will receive power when the Holy Spirit comes on you and you will be my witnesses in Jerusalem, and in all Judea and Samaria, and to the ends of the earth" (Acts 1:8). Jesus knew that this band of locals could not reach the ends of the earth without the limitless power of the Holy Spirit.

On the day of Pentecost, Peter stood up to preach after he received the Holy Spirit. His Spirit-empowered preaching converted three thousand people that day. Ananias told Saul of Tarsus: "Brother Saul, the Lord—Jesus, who appeared to you on the road as you were coming here—has sent me so that you may see again and be filled with the Holy Spirit" (Acts 9:17). Saul needed the power of the Holy Spirit to stand before "the Gentiles and their kings and before the people of Israel" (Acts 9:15).

I have observed the difference between the ministry of highly trained ministers who seemed to lack the power of the Holy Spirit and the ministry of generally unlearned individuals, ministering under the anointing of the Holy Spirit. I must concede that ministry based on training, without the power of the Holy Spirit, is less effective. Paul's description of "having a form of godliness but denying its power" is a real danger in ministry. The world needs authentic, Spirit-filled, and trained ministry.

Theologians who write about ministry seem to neglect the subject of Holy Spirit empowerment. Some will mention this issue but will not clarify its meaning. It is high time to declare that Christian ministers, regardless of their ecclesiastical affiliations, must be filled with the Holy Spirit; there is no substitute for the power of the Holy Spirit in ministry.

Ministers are equipped to lead the people of God under the power of the Holy Spirit. The power of God will manifest in all aspects of ministry. One can preach, teach, heal, and lead by the power of the Holy Spirit. The power of God will also manifest in signs and wonders. The lame will walk (Acts 3:6–7), prison doors will open (Acts 5:17–19), and the divisions between Jew and Gentile, rich and poor, and all other groups will vanish under the power of the Holy Spirit (Acts 10:44–46). The power of God can deliver the oppressed and set the captives free (Acts 16:18, 26).

Power and Powerlessness

Henri Nouwen's book, *The Wounded Healer,* provides a sobering view of ministry.[1] According to Nouwen, a Christian minister is a reflective person—one who reflects theologically on life and its issues. A minister is also active and evocative; he or she does not wait forever; rather he or she initiates. To Nouwen, a Christian minister is an individual who has discovered the voice of the Spirit within him- or herself; in other words, he or she listens to God's voice. A minister is a wounded healer; he or she is one who knows the pain of being hurt, but also one who is in the process of being made whole. Nouwen believes that as we are healed by Christ's stripes (Isa. 53), God can use our wounds as healing resources for others. According to Nouwen, a minister must test everything for biblical authenticity, and he or she must care for him- or herself and for others. A minister must not be afraid to die because he or she is a person of hope. As a person of hope, he or she must also be a person of prayer.

Henri Nouwen's descriptions of ministry, although significant, lack the power dimension of ministry. Certainly, the gospel of Jesus, as Nouwen presents it, contains the mystery of powerlessness. Jesus was not born in a palace, and He did not choose men of power to be His disciples. Jesus did not possess the political and structural power that was characteristic of authority in His day. But through

Christ, God was reconciling the world to Himself. Nouwen is correct when he points out that we often adopt worldly concepts and images of power and overlook the mystery of the power of powerlessness, as found in the kingdom of God. However, the kingdom of God, as it manifests in Spirit-led ministry, is also a mystery. In Spirit-empowered ministry, God's strength is made perfect in our weaknesses. This can happen explicitly in the form of signs, wonders, healing, and miracles. Nouwen does not point this out, but Spirit-empowered ministry can embrace the powerlessness of the cross of Jesus and the power of His resurrection.

Love and Power

Spirit-filled ministry is power-filled ministry. Jesus said, "All authority is given unto me." This authority was given to the disciples who were to continue the ministry of Jesus. Scripture states, "These signs will accompany those who believe." Signs, wonders, and miracles are possible today because the same Spirit that raised Jesus from the dead now dwells in all who belong to Christ (Rom. 8:11). Jesus instructed His disciples not only to preach and teach, but also to heal. Healing is a sign of the kingdom of God as it expands through evangelism and a gift of the Holy Spirit given to God's people. Ministers have the privilege and the authority to pray for healing; whether the approach to ministry is pastoral or evangelistic, a Spirit-led ministry must include healing. In this work, a minister is a steward of God's power.

A minister is a person in dialogue. As mentioned earlier, ministry can be defined as being in dialogue with the world and with God at the same time; a minister communicates simultaneously with God and people. A Spirit-filled minister is an individual who is in love with God and humankind at the same time. Consequently, Spirit-filled ministry must express love for God and love for humanity.

Generally speaking, there are two types of ministry. One overemphasizes love but does not make room for power; the other overemphasizes power but neglects love. A Spirit-filled ministry must maintain equilibrium between these two dimensions.

Revelation and Risk

Spirit-led ministry begins with a revelation of who Christ is. When Peter was confronted with the question, "Who do you say that I am?" he responded, "You are the Christ, the Son of the living God." Jesus told Peter that it was not flesh and blood that revealed this truth to him; it was His Father in heaven. The Samaritan woman who witnessed to her listeners said, "Come, see a man who told me all things that I ever did. Could this be the Christ?" She was at the verge of a revelation as she encountered the Lord Jesus. "Did not our hearts burn within us?" wondered the disciples who met the risen Lord on the Emmaus road as they received the revelation of His identity. This was the beginning of the disciples' ministry of proclamation. Thomas, the apostle to India, had this revelation as he cried out, "My Lord and my God!" Saint Paul's experience was also very similar; he had a sudden revelation of who Jesus was. His first response to the encounter with Jesus was, "Who are you, *Lord*?"

Scripture illustrates that Spirit-led ministry involves risks. When Jesus healed the demoniac, the natives asked Him to depart from their coast. Stephen, who proclaimed the truth to his countrymen, was stoned to death, and Paul found himself left for dead, lowered down a wall in a basket, and locked up in the inner cell of a prison. Spirit-led ministry also requires at times a willingness to risk one's reputation. Jesus was accused of being a friend of tax collectors, and Paul was called a rioter. In spite of all this, Spirit-led ministry produces results. The blind see, the lame walk, the wind and the waves obey, and legions of evil spirits depart.

A minister's affirmation comes from the call of God, not from the external results of ministry. Jesus did not depend on His ministerial results to give Him affirmation. He was affirmed before His first public miracle, when God said, "This is my Son, in whom I am well pleased." Depending on results in order to gain affirmation is a roller coaster ride, because results vary in ministry and what appears to be a failure one day may turn out to be a great success later. Days of triumphant entry are often followed by days of sorrow; escaping danger as a fugitive may follow successful campaigns. Yet God's call and His faithfulness remain unchanging. A minister's affirmation comes from God who called him or her.

Poverty and Prosperity

There has been much misunderstanding in the Christian community regarding what is known as prosperity theology. Simply put, prosperity theology teaches that God wants to bless His children materially. It is unfortunate that this subject has caused so much controversy that some have decided to throw the baby out with the bathwater. It is true that some proponents of this theology have not used wisdom in their teaching, and others have used poor biblical exegesis to establish their doctrine. Yet human fallibility should not cause us to abandon the idea that God is good and that He wants to bless His children in all areas of their lives.

I believe that context has a way of influencing one's theology. For instance, in India I have heard messages glorifying extreme poverty. Reflecting on that doctrine from a distance, I now realize that it had more to do with India's economy and Gandhian philosophy than with the gospel of Jesus Christ. Likewise, in America I have heard extreme messages elevating earthly riches above eternal life. This may reflect the American economic context. I believe that biblical prosperity is different from both of these extremes. In my view, the material prosperity of Christians is a spiritual matter. While material prosperity or poverty is not necessarily evidence of one's spiritual maturity or lack of it, God does bless His children in all areas of their lives. It is not difficult to establish that wherever the gospel is accepted, the social status of the population rises. Some of the wealthiest and most highly educated people in India today are children of early Pentecostals, who were generally poor and uneducated people. In India, social indicators, such as literacy and women's health, are greatest where Christians live. Based on this evidence, I can easily believe that the gospel elevates its followers. My own family has had such an experience.

The Bible speaks against the love of money, not against money itself. This issue seems to center around the difference between controlling and being controlled; does the person control the money or is the opposite true? Does he or she give to those in need? Jesus has both rich and poor followers. Some, like Mother Teresa's Sisters of Charity, choose to be poor. Just as the Bible does not specifically explain the issue of the suffering of innocent people, scripture does not give simple explanations of material poverty. One thing is sure: Jesus came to announce good news to the poor. For these individuals, the message that they no longer have to be poor is truly good news. I do not believe that we should limit riches simply to the spiritual dimension of life. Spirit-led ministers should preach a *balanced* message of biblical prosperity, as they announce the good news to people of all levels of economic status.

Authority of God's Son

Spirit-filled ministry operates in the authority of Jesus, but authentic ministry is often challenged on the basis of its authority. Jesus was questioned many times about His authority. People who knew His background wondered how He dared to do the things

He did. They wanted to know who authorized Him. Ministry still faces this challenge in modern society. Spirit-filled ministry claims its authority from Jesus; a minister needs to know the kind of authority Jesus continues to possess today.

Upon entering Jerusalem, Jesus went into the temple and cleansed it. His words and deeds were very assertive, and His entry into Jerusalem stirred the city. People asked, "Who is this?" (Matt. 21:10). On a different occasion, the disciples asked, "Who is this?" (Luke 8:25). The cleansing of the temple provided an answer to this question in the book of Matthew. Jesus was the one with authority over the temple in order to claim it as a house of prayer; He had more authority than the high priest and the other officers of the temple. Luke, in chapter 8, answers the disciples' question in a similar way. We can summarize the issue as follows.

1. Jesus Has Authority over Natural Forces

While Jesus and the disciples were sailing across the Sea of Galilee, Jesus fell asleep. A great storm arose, which put them in grave danger, so the disciples cried out to Jesus and woke Him up. He rebuked the wind and the waves, and they obeyed Him. Luke testifies of Jesus's authority over natural forces, which even included calming the stormy seas!

2. Jesus Has Authority over Demonic Forces

Luke went on to report the healing of a demon-possessed man in the region of the Gadarenes. This man was living in the tombs, naked and deranged, but when he met Jesus, he fell at His feet. "Jesus asked him, 'What is your name?' 'Legion,' he replied, because many demons had gone into him. And they begged him repeatedly not to order them to go into the Abyss" (Luke 8:30, 31). Jesus gave the demons permission to go into the herd of pigs. The herd rushed into the lake and drowned, but the man who was set free sat at the feet of Jesus "dressed and in his right mind." According to Luke, Jesus has authority over demonic forces. They tremble at His presence and obey Him.

3. Jesus Has Authority over Sickness

Luke reports that upon Jesus's return a great crowd greeted Him and almost crushed Him. A particular woman in that crowd had been suffering from chronic bleeding for twelve years. Physicians could not heal her, and she was desperate. As this nameless woman came up behind Jesus and touched the edge of His garment, she was instantly healed. "Who touched me?" Jesus asked. "Someone touched me; I know that power has gone out of me," He added. The woman came forward, fell at His feet, and gave her testimony. "Daughter, your faith has healed you. Go in peace" (Luke 8:48). In these passages, Luke presents evidence that Jesus has authority over sickness and even over incurable diseases.

4. Jesus Has Authority over Death

The eighth chapter of Luke's gospel ends with the story of Jesus raising the daughter of a man named Jairus, a synagogue ruler. While Jesus was ministering to the woman in the crowd who had just been healed, word came to Jairus that his beloved daughter was dead. Jesus said to Jairus, "Don't be afraid; just believe, and she will be healed" (Luke 8:50). Jesus went to Jairus's house and raised the twelve-year-old girl from the dead. "Her spirit returned, and at once she stood up," (Luke 8:55). In this account, Luke presents evidence of Jesus's ultimate authority, which extends even over the last enemy, death.

Matthew concludes his gospel with the words of Jesus: "All authority in heaven and on earth has been given to me. Therefore go and make disciples of all nations, baptizing them in the name of the Father and of the Son and of the Holy Spirit, and teaching them to obey everything I have commanded you. And surely I am with you always, to the very end of the age" (Matt. 28:18–20). When questioned about authority, this is what a minister needs to remember: Jesus has all authority, and He has given it to His disciples who are called to represent His kingdom. When one ministers in His name, His presence and authority are granted. Spirit-filled ministry is based on the authority of Jesus Christ, the one who calls and commissions His ministers.

Authority of God's Word

We have discussed the minister's authority based on the call of God and the name of Jesus; however, the authority of the Bible as the Word of God is the foundation of all other claims of authority. A Spirit-filled minister must believe that the Bible is the written Word of God, just as Jesus is the living word of God. Only such a conviction can enable a minister to proclaim the Word of God with authority and power. This is not an easy task in this age of relativism and multiculturalism. The New Age religion considers tolerance to be the highest virtue. Taken to an extreme, this means that ultimate truth is negotiable and all religious books have the same significance and level of authority. A Spirit-filled minister cannot agree with this supposedly enlightened position.

God inspired the Bible; it is God-breathed, and it has authority to command our obedience. While the scriptures of other religions have their places in history, as far as a Spirit-filled Christian minister is concerned, the Bible holds a unique position as the Word of God. It contains the whole truth and provides the whole counsel of God.

During my student days, Howard Ervin, professor of Old Testament at Oral Roberts University, helped my understanding of this issue. He said that we must believe the Bible to be the Word of God for the following reasons:

1) Internal witness: The Bible says that it is the Word of God.
2) Historical witness: The church has said for two thousand years that the Bible is the word of God.
3) Personal witness: The Bible has changed my personal life.
4) Existential witness: Preaching and teaching the Bible produces the same results today as it did two thousand year ago.
5) Spiritual witness: The Spirit of God is bearing witness with my spirit that the Bible is the Word of God.

These testimonies are not proof statements. They do not attempt to say that the Bible is a science or history textbook, although much science and history can be found in the Bible. These five statements support me as I take a step of faith to confess that the Bible is the Word of God, which requires my obedience.

One's convictions regarding the Word of God are always revealed in one's teaching and preaching. I cannot imagine a minister performing life-transforming ministry of preaching, teaching, and counseling if he or she has hesitations about the inspiration and authority of the Bible.

A Spirit-Empowered Church

The New Testament word for church is *ecclesia*, which means the assembly of those who are called; the word does not imply a building or a place of assembly. It involves people who are related to one another, not by being in one place, but by being connected to each other through the Head—Jesus Christ. The Bible calls the church by several names, such as the bride of Christ, the body of Christ, family, the household of faith, and the temple of the Holy Spirit.

The church is to be a different kind of community; it is to be a community of faith, transformed by the power of the Holy Spirit and not conforming to this world. Jesus's teaching on the kingdom of God set the pattern that the church is to follow. The kingdom follows a different order from that of the world. As stated earlier, the first shall be last, the last shall be first, giving is the way to receive, and dying is the way to live in the kingdom of God! The church is called to be filled with the Spirit and led by the Spirit, so that it may exemplify this new order through the grace of God and the power of the Holy Spirit.

Jesus Christ is the founder of the church. His own words testify to this truth when He says, "I will build my church." Therefore, any definition of the church must conform to the word of God. The church is a congregation of the faithful who are called by God to join His family; they are called to be followers of Jesus of Nazareth, the Son of the living God. The church must preach the Word of God, administer the ordinances, and facilitate the worship of God and fellowship of the saints. God calls all members of the church. They are adopted into His family and are set apart as priests for the purposes of God. Believers are to be led by the Holy Spirit to be a people of faith, hope, and love.

The church has an organizational dimension, but it is truly a living organism. Any healthy living organism will grow and develop; in the same manner the church must also grow and develop. God's Word and His Spirit sustain the life of the church.

The church has been saved in order to serve. God uses His apostles, prophets, evangelists, pastors, and teachers for the equipping of the believers to perform this work of service.

The church is called to worship, evangelize, fellowship, and show mercy to the needy. According to the last words of Jesus, the mission of the church is to go into *all* of the world, preach to *all* nations, and teach them to obey *all* things commanded by Him. Generally speaking, the church is to continue the work of Jesus by engaging in preaching, teaching, and healing. God loves His church and gives firm warning to those who would try to destroy it; He will not allow the gates of hell to prevail against His church.

The church of Jesus Christ is a community of hope. We are hope-bearers, and Christ in us is the hope of glory. Our hope is not in some date or event; it is in the person of the Lord Jesus Christ who lived, died, was buried, and rose again. He has ascended to heaven and is seated at the right hand of His Father. The hope of the church is that He will come again to receive the church. While no one knows the day or the hour of His coming, one thing is certain: "So shall we ever be with the Lord." The church lives in this eschatological hope and shares that hope with the world in word and deed. The church is a leaven of hope in this world. It is a reminder that God has a plan for His world and that His plan will be accomplished. The church is also a herald, who invites people into the kingdom of God and announces the coming of the King. The church, by its very nature, is a sign to the entire world that God is present in the world and He is at work.

Caring and Meeting Needs

A Spirit-empowered church is a caring community, and yet the "backdoor phenomenon" remains a major concern of megachurches.

A significant number of the people who come in through the front door of these churches leave through the back door. I believe that this is mainly due to inadequate pastoral care of the people. Many churches do not have an adequate pastoral care plan, which leads them to either ignore congregational needs or use untrained individuals to meet pastoral care needs. Although there are exceptions, most of the untrained individuals are not able to meet the needs of the people. While all can testify that the pastoral care needs of even a small church cannot be fully met by the lead pastor, he or she must be responsible to ensure that the shepherding needs of the people are met by well-trained individuals who have a calling to care for others. Unfortunately, in many churches even the staff members do not feel pastored. Their staff meetings may be more administrative than pastoral. Sometimes even care group planning meetings are primarily administrative in nature.

The church needs to understand the true meaning of 2 Corinthians 1:3–4: "Praise be to the God and Father of our Lord Jesus Christ, the Father of compassion and the God of all comfort, who comforts us in all our troubles, so that we can comfort those in any trouble with the comfort we ourselves have received from God." Care and comfort begin with God; one must receive care and then pass it on to others. This means that the senior pastor must truly care for his or her associates, and the associates ought to genuinely care for the care group leaders. Care group leaders need to pass on what they receive to the people under their care. Three or more levels of administration should be replaced with three or more levels of caring; there must be care beyond administration and hierarchy. Caring in this manner will close the back doors of many churches.

People come to church with diverse needs. Plans and programs should be in place to meet the multitude of needs represented among the members. Consider Abraham Maslow's hierarchy of human needs to examine this concern. According to Maslow, the needs of human beings exist on different levels.[2] Physiological and survival needs constitute the lowest level. Above this level is the need for safety, which is followed by love and belongingness needs. Self-esteem needs follow belongingness needs, but the highest level of human need is the need for what Maslow calls self-actualization.

I agree with Maslow that human needs are distributed on various levels; however, due to the strong secular connotations of the term *self-actualization*, I would like to consider the idea of kingdom lifestyle. In my view, kingdom lifestyle manifests when an individual actualizes his or her fullest potential in God. In other words, when a believer fulfills God's purpose for his or her life, he or she is truly actualizing. Kingdom lifestyle involves a life guided by the values of the kingdom of God and lived in the power of the Holy Spirit. As we have emphasized before, kingdom values appear to be upside down—the first will be the last, dying is the way to live, and giving is the avenue to receive.

I refer to Maslow's model not to defend a secular model, but to challenge the church to address the totality of human needs. Instead of teaching and preaching as if the totality of human need exists at the lowest, or physiological, level of the hierarchy of needs and having programs and forums to meet only these perceived needs, expand the assessment of needs and develop additional ministries to address the higher level needs. Make developing kingdom citizens the ultimate goal of ministries. Although parachurch ministries can address selected needs, a Spirit-filled church would be remiss to address only one level of need. Many churches do not assess the total needs of the congregation and design ministries to meet those needs. This situation is not healthy.

Preaching and teaching that respond to the totality of human needs, emphasizing kingdom principles and kingdom lifestyle, are desperately needed in the churches. Churches must intentionally design effective programs to address the higher level needs of their members. Only such churches will produce strong disciples of Jesus in this generation. A Spirit-empowered church is a need-meeting church. This is not an effort to advance a strictly program-driven church. Even a church with excellent programming should give priority to what the Spirit of God is calling it to do in ministry.

Evangelizing

The disciples were empowered to evangelize. Sharing the good news with those who have not heard it is at the heart of the gospel. The gospel in one word is "Come!" And Jesus's parting message to His followers in one word was "Go!" The church is empowered to go and tell the nations. Modern technology has made going much easier, but the western church seems to be unsure of its message. However, the Spirit-empowered movement, most of it spread out in the global South, is the fastest growing segment of Christianity today. This represents empowered evangelism true to its New Testament roots, in spite of its idiosyncrasies. More than 700 million people consider themselves Spirit-filled today. Compare this with the number of people who made this claim in 1901! One can only conclude that God has not forgotten His plans for humanity. It is humbling to realize that representatives of this group were not even present at the strategic mission conference held in Edinburgh in 1910!

Evangelism is enhanced by signs and wonders. Signs and wonders are not human inventions. God confirms His Word through signs, wonders, healings, and miracles. It is well documented that people are witnessing these in many parts of the world. An empowered church preaches the gospel in faith, and God does the rest. A truly empowered church cannot inhibit evangelism through extreme measures of user friendliness. The foolishness of preaching cannot be made completely seeker friendly.

Whether we live in America or another part of the world, we do not live in the world in which we were born; in this sense, we are all immigrants. As immigrants, we struggle to adjust to our new world. Born in the age of horse and buggy and steam engine trains, many of us now live in the age of supersonic jets and space vehicles. Remember when we had to travel to distant places to deliver some important news? Today, with wireless phones, satellite communication facilities, social media, and other high tech means, people no longer depend on the old ways. We must discover new forms of evangelization.

Seven Forces

I believe that the following seven forces are shaping the modern world and effective evangelism must address them.

1. *Science and Technology*

The strongest force impacting our world is technology. It has moved us from old typewriters to new technologies. Television, cell phones, the Internet, and many other inventions have changed our entire way of life. Some time ago, a *National Geographic* reporter described the glowing television sets in the homes of slum-dwelling families in Mumbai, who had access to a multitude of television channels.[3] Today, even beggars in India have cellphones and debit cards! Technology is enslaving and liberating modern humankind at the same time. We are able to connect with the world in numerous ways now, but find ourselves very isolated and lonely. We chat more but converse less. People know our profile but not us. Our children used to play ball outdoors; they now sit for hours and stare at various screens, monitors, and tablets. Technology provides unique challenges and opportunities. The fields of education, health care, and entertainment have drastically changed as a result of changing technologies. Ministers must find new and creative ways to harness technology to address the problems and to evangelize.

2. *Knowledge*

Information is the second force shaping today's world. The Internet has created an information superhighway. Knowledge is flowing in full color on the Internet, allowing one to log on from anywhere and study any subject at any time. We are raising a generation that has access to information without supervision. Unfortunately, we have increasing knowledge, but we lack wisdom; we have information, but we do not know how to evaluate it. We lack the skill to discern between what is good and what is not, and what is real and what is fake.

3. *Cultural Change and Speed of Life*

The world is changing so fast that many people feel like riders on a roller coaster. Easy access to technology and multimedia and increasing opportunities for global travel are enabling people to incorporate features of faraway cultures into their own. Old preachers in India are clad in western suits, while young Americans wear nose rings! Cultural barriers are being removed. Unfortunately, some have adopted all new trends, while others resist all changes. Violence has become common, terrorism has expanded, ethnic cleansing has entered the vocabulary, and time has become a rare commodity. In a world with instant coffee, instant meetings, and even instant weddings, cultures are changing and fusing so rapidly, creating a world culture. Unable to cope with the speed of life and many accompanying losses, a counterculture is also developing across the western world that resists globalization, immigration, and loss of values.

4. *New Spirituality*

Fed up with materialism, yet enslaved by it, the world has adopted a new spirituality. This spirituality is generally defined by the absence of a Holy God. Modern humankind believes in a nebulous spiritual force. Instead of acknowledging God the Father, God the Son, or God the Holy Spirit, the New Age religion mixes Hinduism, Buddhism, Christianity, and aspects of various other religions. Ayurveda (Eastern medicine) and transcendental meditation are sold as spirituality in America, and even extreme environmentalism has become a religion for some. Today's pseudo spirituality has no Ten Commandments or Sermon on the Mount to guide it; it affirms all alternate lifestyles, and tolerance of everything is its highest moral value.

5. *Broken Families*

Families are breaking down on Main Street, USA. Families, regardless of their race and economic status, are in distress. At one time, Asians could brag about their strong families; even non-Christian Asians had strong family ties. This is not the case anymore; many Asian families are falling apart. Working parents have little time for their children, and the earphones stuck in the youth's ears and the digital tablets they are staring at prevent them from hearing their parents' words even when the family is together.

6. *Money God*

The love of money has always existed, but the current culture has taken that concept to new heights. While the Great Recession of the twenty-first century has deprived a generation of young people of decent employment and dignity, some are willing to do anything for a few dollars. Keeping up with the Joneses requires a lot of borrowing, and many cannot afford to pay back their debts. Greed is not new, but the current culture has normalized it and made it a virtue. Some parents have few values to give their children, only unpredictable stocks. We seem to have learned very little from the Great Recession of the twenty-first century.

7. *Hopelessness*

This is a hopeless age. There are new epidemics threatening the world, and heart disease and cancer are still medical challenges. The gap between the rich and the poor is widening. Terrorism has become a global concern. Suicide bombers represent the ultimate hopelessness of this age.

A Strategic Proposal for Evangelism

How shall we evangelize the inhabitants of such an age? I believe that our evangelistic efforts must take into account all these forces that are shaping the world. Let me propose some ideas for Spirit-empowered churches to include in a strategic plan for evangelism in the twenty-first century.

1. *Use Technology*

Use technology to spread the gospel. Since multimedia and the Internet are today's marketplaces, we can bring the message of the gospel to these popular forums as eagerly as we brought it to the marketplaces through open-air meetings, radio, and television. We must not compromise the gospel, but be willing to change our evangelistic methods.

2. *Increase Ministerial Education*

Train ministers at a higher level. The knowledge level of the population is increasing; consequently, ministers must be given better education for ministry. Bible schools and seminaries must move beyond being cottage industries. Bible schools that can combine academics with spiritual empowerment and practical skills are needed. Pastors need to learn leadership and management skills and conflict resolution strategies. Seminaries need to reconsider their tendency to produce only teachers and counselors and ensure that theological schools produce practicing pastors and evangelists. Ultimately, theological schools need to produce apostles, prophets, evangelists, pastors, and teachers (Eph. 4).

3. *Design Creative Methods*

Offer spiritually refreshing ministry to people living in today's fast-paced society. Hurting people are attracted by a gospel that heals; therefore, design creative ways to draw their attention to the good news.

4. *Offer Transformation*

Preach the Word and teach biblical spirituality, not just cultural Christianity or irrelevant versions of Pentecostalism. Instead of preaching about trends and fashions, preach Jesus Christ and Him crucified. Emphasize life transformation rather than self-help and religious appearance.

5. Strengthen Families

Attract souls through programs that strengthen marriage and family life. People must be taught how to be good husbands, wives, and parents. Counseling seminars, camp meetings, marriage classes, and parenting seminars are some of the means by which secular people can be attracted to the Lord Jesus. These programs will also benefit believers.

6. Live the Gospel

Practice lifestyle evangelism. A Christian's lifestyle must reflect his or her faith; let the preaching and practice match. Live as if Christ is one's treasure, not material things. This requires that believers be taught to share material goods with others in need and to give tithes and offerings. Giving is not just for Westerners; all God's people must be givers. For this to happen, pastors must teach the blessings of giving in the name of Jesus. There must be ways and means to assist unbelievers in need as part of evangelism.

7. Update Spiritual Vocabulary

A study of young people commissioned by Oral Roberts University revealed that they wish to see (a) authentic leadership, (b) sincere mentoring, and (c) a new vocabulary to express old biblical truths. It appears that the current generation in charge of spiritual matters has corrupted the vocabulary of Spirit-empowered ministry and evangelism. Take the new generation seriously and update our spiritual vocabulary in a way that the young generation can understand and receive the age-old truths.

8. *Offer Hope*

Be people of hope. In order for unbelievers to see real hope in Christ, Christians must adopt a lifestyle based on hope. Allow others to see how disappointments are properly handled; let them see real hope in the midst of crises. People who watch Christians must see Christ, the hope of glory!

9. *Simply Preach the Good News*

Trying to be extremely seeker friendly, some churches have watered down the good news of Jesus Christ. In search of a new vocabulary in good faith, some have abandoned crucial words from the gospel's mother tongue. Sin, hell, and repentance are still important words of the gospel. Be seeker friendly by avoiding words and practices of the Christian subculture, but don't mess with God's message to the people He loves. Preach God's Truth with a capital T.

Making Disciples

Spirit-empowered churches must be disciple-making churches. The development of seeker-friendly and user-friendly churches is an important concern, but efforts to focus only on seeker-friendly services and not on methods to transform seekers into disciples will neglect the work for which we have been called. A Spirit-empowered church must offer intentional paths to discipleship.

I like the model of discipleship that Robert Coleman presents in *The Masterplan of Discipleship*.[4] He outlines how we can transform seekers into disciples, disciples into workers, and workers into leaders. His method is very biblical and practical. Unbelievably, some Charismatic churches do not have any form of Christian education or strategic discipleship plans. A Spirit-filled church must be more than a place of celebration; it must be an incubator in which disciples of Jesus Christ can develop and mature.

The world today desperately needs disciples. The political and business scandals of the new century reveal one thing very clearly: There is a great need for ethical people in today's society. Contemporary political events reveal a lack of ethics at the highest levels of government. How many chief executive officers of megacorporations are hauled off to the Capitol because they disregarded ethics? Shocked by these situations, ethics courses are now mandatory in business schools across the nation. But this remedial work should not be left to business schools; the church must do its part and make disciples. Society needs people who practice Christian ethics and kingdom principles

The time has come to develop character-forming churches. Charismatic churches give much attention to the gifts of the Holy Spirit, but there is a need to place equal emphasis on the fruits of the Spirit. The fruits of the Spirit are listed in Galatians 5:22–23: love, joy, peace, patience, kindness, goodness, faithfulness, gentleness, and self-control. These are character qualities. God bestows the gifts, but the fruits need to be cultivated through time and discipline. The church ought to assist people in this cultivation through discipleship. No quick fixes apply in this area; this requires strategic changes. Keep in mind that only a disciple-making church can be a character-forming church.

Organism and Organization

The concept of management as a part of ministry has brought confusion in many circles. As a result, the language of business is replacing biblical and theological vocabulary in many churches and ministries across the world. Terms like market share, marketing, public relations, needs analysis, customer satisfaction, environmental scanning, strategic plan, change management, efficiency, branding, and so forth are replacing evangelism, discipleship, compassion, Christian education, faith promise, caring, and the like in many places. A similar change in church vocabulary took place a generation ago when psychology made its way into the churches and provided an additional model of pastoral ministry and a new image of pastor as therapist.

Business concepts are important and can certainly contribute to the efficient operation of the organizational aspects of the community of faith. The problem is that the border between business and businesslike is disappearing in a fast pace. No, some unscrupulous people are not responsible for this. It is actually the result of good people with very good intentions applying excellent business concepts to the body of Christ without adequate biblical and theological reflection. They are simply adapting good business principles and practices without baptizing them.

Here's the problem: the church is not simply an organization; it is primarily a living organism. The Bible does not dwell on the organizational aspects of the church; instead, it uses familial language to describe the church. The church is the family of God, the community of faith, the body of Christ, and the household of faith. A family is not about bottom line. It is about relationships and stewardship. It is a place of sacrifices and nurturing, not profit, profit-sharing, customer satisfaction, and normal concepts of return on investment.

No doubt, the church has always been involved with the marketplace. Marketplace must be a context of ministry and a contributor to missions. However, the church is not simply a business. The difference between business and businesslike must be preserved in the context of the church and its ministries.

Three business concepts have contributed to the confusion in this regard—leadership, change, and efficiency. These are the troublesome assumptions behind these concepts: everyone must be a leader, all changes are good and needed, and efficiency is the highest value in all situations. Let's briefly examine these.

Leadership: The Bible says very little about leadership as this concept is understood in today's society. The scripture talks much more about *followership*! "Leader" is not a frequent word in the Bible. We are advised to remember our leaders and to imitate their faith, but we are called to take up the cross and follow Jesus. God calls certain people to lead others, but the spirit in which they lead is not arrogance; it is service. In the kingdom of God, leaders are not CEOs; they are servants and followers at the same time. Biblical leaders are to invite others to follow them only as they follow Christ. Not everyone should be a leader in the body of Christ. It is okay to be a follower in the family of God.

Change: Although institutions must be flexible enough to adapt to changes around them, the idea that constant change is what is needed in all situations is not true. Some changes are unnecessary and damaging. Some things should be left alone. There is no need to repair unbroken things.

Efficiency: Efficiency is a good thing, but there are higher values than efficiency in some situations. A grandmother may not be the most efficient member of the family, but do you want to replace her? Tithing may not be the most efficient financial management by some measures, but do you want to stop giving to God? Raising children is not the most efficient way to spend money, but do you want to disown your children? No, certainly not. Efficiency is important, but sometimes there are other values that are more important. Relationships matter. Compassion matters. Here's the truth: sometimes ministry is inefficient.

So here I stand. The church is not a business, but its organizational aspects must be operated like a business. Many churches and ministries are guilty of sloppy and sometimes illegal operations and business practices. Applying excellent business practices to the organizational dimension of the church is good Christian stewardship, but great caution must be taken not to blur the lines between the life and mission of the body of Christ and its operational responsibilities. The church of Jesus Christ in the world today is both an organism and an organization at the same time. The organization must serve the organism. It should never be the other way.

Under Authority and Accountable

Spirit-empowered churches need leaders who are under authority and accountable. Pastors need administrative authority to conduct the operational affairs of their churches. A church's particular ecclesiology underlies the kind of authority its pastor exercises. One must avoid two extreme forms of exercising authority. The first involves a board or committee that keeps all administrative power to itself so that the pastor cannot implement the vision God has given him or her. In this type of churches the pastor is simply a hired hand. Some individuals on these boards are often controllers who feel that God has called them to keep the preacher poor and humble. On the other hand, some pastors are dictators who are not accountable to any human person or group. Since pastors are human beings with normal human weaknesses, this is a risky situation for all parties concerned.

All ministers need accountability. The pastoral epistles list the required characteristics for people who are called to leadership positions in the church. The book of Acts records that the apostles were accountable for their lifestyles and for their doctrines. Ministerial ethics also requires meaningful accountability. Ministers invite deception by surrounding themselves with individuals who are afraid of them and who may benefit from their indiscretions. What they really need are spiritual fathers and elders who will grant them freedom, authority, and accountability. Many pastors have crashed and burned due to a lack of caring people in their lives who could speak the truth in love to them. This is an avoidable problem; instead of waiting for problems to develop, pastors and leaders should initiate the establishment of an accountability system for their own protection.

Portrait of a Healthy Congregation

Pastoral theologian Charles Gerkin described the five characteristics of a healthy Christian congregation. Pentecostal and Charismatic churches will benefit from examining themselves in light of Gerkin's categories. According to him, a healthy church is a (1) community of language, (2) a community of memory, (3) a community of inquiry, (4) a community of mutual care, and (5) a community of mission.[5] A healthy church is one that aspires to be a *Spirit-filled* community of language, memory, inquiry, mutual care, and mission.

1. A Community of Language

The language that Gerkin refers to is not any particular native language, nor is it Pentecostal tongues; it has to do with the language, images, and metaphors contained in the Bible. According to Gerkin, a church must become a community that uses biblical language, images, and metaphors. The Word of God should form and inform a church's worldview.

The power of biblical images to form a worldview can be illustrated with the following example. The Bible contains the history of God's people in migration as well as exile. Migration and exile are two different things; while exiles are forced to live the way they do, migrants make a choice. These biblical images can help us understand ourselves better as aliens and pilgrims in this world who are called to look for a city whose builder and maker is God.

2. A Community of Memory

A community of memory is one that remembers its past and focuses on the ways in which the Lord has brought it thus far. Christians are instructed not to forget all God's benefits (Ps. 103:2). God is not pleased when His people forget His mercies.

There are those among the people of God who have forgotten how God brought them from the wrong side of the tracks to a place of honor. The community of faith must not forget its past and what the Lord has done for it. Moreover, a church should teach its young about their spiritual heritage; it must find ways to keep the memory of God's dealings with it alive.

3. A Community of Inquiry

University students often say that the Charismatic community discourages them from pursuing education. This is especially true of mature theological students. Many think that only young people should be learners and ignore the fact that the whole world is moving toward the concept of lifelong learning. This is especially true in North America. All major corporations are supportive of employees' quest for lifelong learning. The world is changing so quickly, and new information is generated so rapidly that unless one remains a student for life, it is impossible to excel in any field.

The old Sunday-school-is-for-kids mentality must change in the Charismatic community. All must become students of the Word of God. Ignorance does not glorify God. Jesus did not die on the cross to wash away our brains!

The opportunity to be a student should not be limited to young adulthood; many user-friendly options for learning exist today. Ministers must take advantage of these and encourage other adult learners. The average seminary student in North America is in his or her thirties now; these individuals have discovered that learning is the best form of investment.

Some Christians fear that education will kill their desire for spiritual things. It is time to get beyond the fear of education; there are numerous living examples around to prove that learning does not kill one's enthusiasm for spiritual things. It is possible, as Oral Roberts said, to "get your learning and keep your burning."

4. A Community of Mutual Care

To ensure a good future for all its members, the Christian community must find ways to care for one another. In order to become a truly caring community, everyone ought to seek the well-being of others in the name of Christ. God has promised that for those who seek His Kingdom first, all the other things shall be given (Matt. 6:33). As a person cares for others, God's care will flow to him or her through multiple avenues. Ultimately, a healthy church is a caring community.

Although many churches are growing, not all of them are providing adequate spiritual support for their people. Healthy churches train their members, formally and informally, to assist others who are struggling with various problems and needs.

5. A Community of Mission

American Charismatics need a mission strategy that is bigger than themselves. This may be true of churches outside the United States also. Generally speaking, Charismatics have been too shortsighted in their strategy for world missions. Although short-term missions are a part of God's plan, one should not assume that God has exempted everyone from all long-term commitments. Charismatics can learn from Catholic, Southern Baptist, and Assemblies of God missionary programs that long-term commitment of personnel and resources to particular geographical locations or people groups can make long-lasting positive changes. This is particularly true when indigenous individuals are trained for continuing leadership in ministry.

A healthy church is also concerned about the lost and dying. It is committed to reaching the world with the gospel of Jesus Christ at any cost. The gospel is global and must be shared with the whole world. God wants His church to be a healthy one in memory, in language, in inquiry, in mutual care, and in missions. Blessed is the pastor who leads a healthy church!

From a Spirit-empowered perspective, two significant characteristics are missing from Gerkin's list: spiritual worship and sacrificial giving. Gerkin may include worship as part of the memory, but spiritual worship deserves its own place in demonstrating a healthy church. The body of Christ is called to worship God in spirit and in truth. Worship invokes the presence of God, and God's power manifests where He is present. Also, a healthy church is a giving church. Members of the congregation in healthy churches give their time, talent, and treasures to bless their communities, especially those in the household of faith, both locally and globally.

In his book *Your Church Can Grow*, Peter Wagner lists seven vital signs of a healthy church.[6] According to Wagner, a healthy church has a positive pastor who is full of faith and optimism. It also has a well-mobilized laity and gives priority to meeting the needs of its members. A healthy church gives its members multiple opportunities for belonging; people need to be part of the gathering for celebration. They also need a sense of belonging to the congregation, the active community of faith, at that place. A small group, in which people can experience intimate belonging, is also important. This intimate context can provide the accountability and growth opportunities that each believer needs.

Wagner also supports the controversial idea of homogeneous groups. He believes that having a particular social, economic, and racial majority is an important aspect of a healthy church. He believes that effective evangelistic methods and biblical priorities are also important for the health of the church.

In his book *Pastor as Priest*, Ronald Sunderland lists six elements of congregational growth and health.[7] According to Sunderland, a healthy church has a common identity and shares a common authority. A growing church shares a common memory, which includes the memory of the life, death, and resurrection of Jesus, as well as the local memory of the congregation. Christians must regularly tell the stories of the church in order to keep the memories alive and to allow the newest members to become part of the story. Sunderland adds that a growing church has a common vision. A house divided against itself cannot prosper, but a common vision keeps the family of faith together. A growing congregation shares its life among its members, and it shares its life with the world.

The healthy church described in the book of Acts is a Spirit-empowered church. It is both Spirit-filled and Spirit-led. As discussed elsewhere in this book, the church in Acts is primarily a praying church. Much of the book of Acts describes the apostles praying or going to prayer meetings (Acts 1:14, 4:31). The earnest prayer of the church on behalf of Peter in prison is recorded in detail (Acts 12:5). A Spirit-empowered church is a united church, as the Spirit moves where people are in unity (Acts 2:1). A Spirit-filled church is also a fellowshipping church (Acts 2:42) and a giving church (Acts 2:44–45). Since doctrines are important for every living church, a Spirit-led church should also be involved in teaching and learning (Acts 2:42, 17:11). The book of Acts demonstrates that a Spirit-filled church is a living organism; it grows and multiplies. The church in Acts added to and multiplied its membership regularly (Acts 2:41, 47, 6:1). The first Spirt-empowered church emphasized praise and worship. A Spirit-led minister will lead the church to grow in all these qualities.

Chapter 4
Empowered and Competent Ministry

> Do your best to present yourself to God as one
> approved, a worker who does not need to be ashamed
> and who correctly handles the word of truth.
> —2 Timothy 2:15

Some within the charismatic community consider the word *professional* inappropriate to describe a Spirit-led minister. I disagree because I use the word *professional* to mean one who has a theory for his practice. A Christian minister's theory is theology. A good professional is one who has a reason for what he or she does and a basis for his or her actions. Imitation should not be the only model for Spirit-empowered ministry. Ministers must be informed practitioners even as they are fully open to the empowerment and leading of the Holy Spirit. Spirit-empowered ministers must actually be reflective practitioners. Their work in ministry must be based on the Word of God. It must be empowered and led by the Holy Spirit and informed by the history of the church and an understanding of their contexts.

Competent Ministries

Spirit-filled ministers need particular competencies to be effective in today's culture. Whether one is a pastor, chaplain, or evangelist, certain knowledge, attitude, and skills are required to deliver excellence in ministry. We will now look at some specialized ministries in and out of the church.

Ministry to Families

American families are in desperate need of focused ministry today. The high rate of divorce and increased violence in homes and schools demand competent ministry to families. Often the church's ministry assumes that all members come from traditional nuclear families; however, statistics do not support this assumption. Worshipers and church members today represent all types of families. Many are from single-parent homes, households headed by single women, or families in which children are parented by grandparents. Ministers require a special understanding of the needs of these men, women, and children.

Many cultural misunderstandings exist regarding marriage and family. The following is a partial list of such misconceptions:

1) Marriage is a contract, not a covenant.
2) Contracts have deadlines; they are not necessarily for life.
3) Marriage is a partnership, not a union.
4) The basic idea behind marriage is the concept of significant other.
5) A spouse is a domestic partner.
6) In marriage, convenience is more important than conviction.
7) Family life and cohabitation are the same.

8) Childbearing and lifestyle-based optional surrogate mothering are the same.
9) Material things are more important than the marital relationship.
10) Marriage should be tolerated, not celebrated.

Ministers must keep in mind that the only constant thing in family life is change. Just as individuals go through life stages, marriage also goes through predictable stages. Herbert Anderson in *The Family and Pastoral Care* offers the following model of the stages of family development:

1) Forming the family (newlyweds)
2) Enlarging the family (children are born)
3) Expanding the family (children's world expands through friends)
4) Extending the family (in-laws are added)
5) Reforming the family[1] (original couple)

Essentially, this model affirms that families are always changing. Ministry must address this constant change, as well as the people positioned in each stage. Through reading and theological reflection, ministers can better understand the complex needs and issues of the people in these stages.

Ministers must also address the unhealthy state of many marriages in today's society. In his book *A Marital Therapy Manual*, psychiatrist Peter A. Martin says that there are four types of sick marriages:

1) Deprived marriages where one feels deprived by the other partner.
2) Marriages in which one of the partners, particularly the husband, is in search of a mother.

3) The double parasite marriage, where both partners are exploiting each other.
4) The paranoid marriage, where the couple is fearful of everyone else and believes that people are actually working against them.

Martin lists the qualities of healthy marriage partners as follows:

1) Capacity for independence and interdependence
2) Capacity to support one's mate
3) Capacity to accept support
4) Capacity to have physical intimacy
5) Capacity to have emotional intimacy[2]

Ministry must address the need for healing in sick and broken marriages. Ministers can meet the various needs through preaching, teaching, and counseling as well as through helpful programs sponsored by the church and parachurch organizations.

Although no perfect families exist, we must encourage families to be as functional and wholesome as possible. The church, as the household of faith, must also be wholesome and functional. Experts have identified several symptoms of dysfunctional families. For instance, in unhealthy families, members are not allowed to have feelings; feelings are neither owned, nor freely expressed. Family members do not trust one another, and the family lacks open communication. In order to avoid speaking unpleasant things, issues are not verbalized. This fosters unhealthy secrets within the family, which eventually undermines the entire family.

According to Herbert Anderson, wholesome families have three healthy areas: (1) roles, (2) rules, and (3) rituals.[3] In a healthy family, each member has a definable role to play, and each functions normally in that role. In crisis, however, members are able to exchange roles in a positive way. Dysfunctional families, on the other hand, have confused roles. Members do not know how to exchange roles based on a given situation. Healthy families also have explicit rules by which they live. Each party in the family knows the rules, but the rules are negotiable. Parents do not wait to explain the rules until their children have broken them. Members can also question outdated rules and renegotiate more appropriate rules. Dysfunctional families live by rigid and often secret rules; they maintain outdated rules and are threatened by any attempts to negotiate them. Family rituals represent healthy habits, because they are predictable and dependable. For example, the family expects that a birthday will be celebrated. Worship is also part of the normal family schedule. Rituals provide security, because everyone in the family knows what to expect.

Unfortunately, some churches are also dysfunctional. Lessons for a healthy family can also be applied to parsonages and churches. Ministers must remember that the most effective ministry occurs when the church provides a healthy model to follow.

Ministers can improve their skills in marriage counseling by taking courses from colleges and seminaries. Specialized degree programs that lead graduates to state licenses as marriage and family therapists are now available across the country. This brief section is to provide some basics to encourage general pastoral care of families. Pastors are encouraged to seek counseling skills or to have trusted counselors to recommend to their church members in need.

Ministry to Women

Ministry to women requires a special understanding of their needs. Pastors should recognize that women face many disadvantages in our society, particularly if they are part of an ethnic minority. Studies show that, on average, a woman pays a higher price for certain products than a man if she goes alone to make the purchase. Products geared specifically toward women often carry a higher price tag. Women are charged a higher price for everything from shampoo to automobiles.

Our culture sends many conflicting messages to women, and the church often inadvertently reinforces these cultural messages. For instance, Christie Neuger identifies several paradoxical messages:

1. You are valuable as a woman because of your nurturing and relational capacities; but as a culture we value independence and autonomy.
2. You must be submissive, patient, and supportive in your family life; yet why have you not left your abusive husband—you must, at some level, like the violence.
3. You can be anything you want to be; however, 60 percent of all females in the work force hold clerical and retail positions, or service jobs, in which at least 75 percent of their colleagues are female.[4]

Women in ministry also report that they face many issues in the church. Theologically liberal women testify that they are oppressed through male-dominated theology, worship, history, polity, leadership, and seminary classrooms. According to Duane Parker of the Association of Clinical Pastoral Education, female clergy are looking for the following:

1) A new form of worship
2) A sense of community
3) Recognition of their contributions
4) A sense of collegiality

5) Equal employment and pay
6) Nonhierarchical polity
7) Ordination regardless of gender[5]

Women's ministry was not a major issue for the early Pentecostals; unfortunately, this cannot be said of today's classical Pentecostals. Happily, women's ministry is much less of a problem for independent Charismatics; the ministries of Joyce Meyers (television ministry), Sharon Daugherty (local pastor in Tulsa, Oklahoma), and others prove this fact. Women in Pentecostal groups find it difficult to be ordained in some denominations, especially if they have any desire to pastor. Most ordained female candidates in these faith groups are parachurch ministers or foreign missionaries. Some scholars believe that the current issues among Pentecostals related to the inspiration of scripture and the ordination of women are problems borrowed more recently from faith groups that have these unresolved issues.

According to Kay Marshal Storm, persons ministering to women in today's culture should be prepared to deal with issues related to the following problems:

1) alcohol and drug abuse
2) child abuse
3) molestation as a child or of a child
4) incest
5) infidelity
6) rape
7) suicide
8) teen pregnancy and unwanted pregnancy
9) wife abuse
10) issues of suffering[6]

Storm gives males the following advice for ministering to women:

1) Don't be physically involved.
2) Don't encourage dependence.
3) Don't force the male perspective.
4) Don't ignore one's own prejudices.

Jesus considered ministry to women very important. He ministered to women and allowed women to minister. Even the apostle Paul, whose words some feminists quote to attack the church, endorsed and praised the ministry of women. The church of Jesus Christ must continue its ministry, part of which is to empower women to minister to others. Ministry in the twenty-first century must include ministry to women and ministry by women. One task of the global church is to discover culturally appropriate ways of involving women in ministry, and to engage them in the process of transforming culture.

It is sad to see certain major faith groups excluding women from public proclamation of the gospel. If this approach is adopted by all Christian faith groups, 500 million Muslim women with strict gender role adherence will not hear the gospel! I hope this situation changes. May Joel's prophecy be fulfilled in our day: "Your sons and your daughters shall prophesy" (Joel 2:28).

Ministry to Children

Children's ministry is a special need in today's church. Senior pastors cannot leave this ministry to a department of the church; all ministers, especially senior pastors, should have a deep understanding of the needs and issues of children today. The fact is that children are neglected in our churches, often due to the unmentionable reason that they are not financial contributors.

Children are frequently idealized and viewed as being free from problems. Many times, childcare is seen as women's work. In reality, pastors lack training in ministry to children, and their feelings of inadequacy keep them away from this ministry. We must remember that the church is the family of God and the household of faith. A family is a place in which every child is valued and cared for. The house of God must not be an exception to this rule.

From a theological perspective, children are significant. The mystery of the incarnation is a sign that children are important to God. The infinite became an infant! Christ exhorts us to be childlike and challenges us to have childlike faith. "Let the little children come to me, and do not hinder them, for the kingdom of God belongs to such as these" (Mark 10:14).

According to Andrew Lester, children need their ministers to offer the following:

1) A sense of competence
2) Positive attitudes and values
3) Confirmation or correction of their perceptions
4) A sense of belonging
5) A friend and a hero to look up to
6) Listening ears
7) Acceptance of their feelings
8) Spiritual guidance[7]

Lester believes many methods are available to minister to children, such as play, art, and storytelling.

The Gospels illustrate that Jesus was concerned about children, and that He was comfortable with them. He healed and blessed children, even to the point of aggravating the disciples. The church must continue this tradition of ministry that values little children. The Catholic Church faced serious charges against their priests at the beginning of the twenty-first century regarding their treatment of children. However, neglect or abuse of children is not just a Catholic problem, it is a Christian problem. Modern society contains enough threats against children; even schools have become dangerous places. All servants of God must participate in the nurturing of children, so that the house of God can be a safe haven and a place of healing for all the children of the world.

Institutional Ministry/Chaplaincy

While ministers in the Spirit-empowered movement have sought expertise in church planting and church growth, until recently they neglected the potential of institutional ministry. Institutional ministries include military chaplaincy, health-care chaplaincies, industrial chaplaincies, and other forms of ministry not directly related to the local church. It appears that American Pentecostals appreciate the need for long-term foreign missions, whereas Charismatics specialize in short-term overseas missions. However, both groups have a difficult time seeing the tremendous needs and ministry opportunities that exist in the major institutions of this country.

Traditionally, these institutional ministries have been dominated by mainline Protestants. The mainline faith groups have organizational structures in place to supervise the training of candidates and endorse them for these ministries. Pentecostal denominations, such as the Assemblies of God and Church of God, saw the potential for these ministries first, but Charismatics are also beginning to see the need. Colonel Jim Ammerman was a pioneer in promoting Charismatic ministry in the armed forces. He started the Chaplaincy of the Full Gospel Churches organization and was very active in recruiting and assisting seminarians with their military chaplaincy placements.

Institutional ministry requires special professional preparation. I will present only a brief description of that process here. Education and training are the first requirements. Most professional ministry positions in institutional settings require a Master of Divinity degree, which is a three-year post-baccalaureate degree. Normally, the degree must be earned at a seminary that is professionally accredited by the Association of Theological Schools in the United States and Canada (ATS). Additionally, a candidate must receive ordination by a recognized faith community. It can be a local church, denomination, or network of churches. Most chaplaincy positions in hospitals, prisons, and the military require an additional endorsement from the proper authority of a particular faith community. Denominations have their boards and commissions to do this work. Independent Charismatics can now work with organizations such as the Chaplaincy of Full Gospel Churches.

Clinical training beyond the Master of Divinity is required for many professional positions. The best training is called Clinical Pastoral Education (CPE). The Association for Clinical Pastoral Education (ACPE) offers training for seminary students and graduates across the United States. This organization has a rich history and offers training at basic, advanced, and supervisory levels in hospitals, clinics, and other centers. The training includes practical experience, classroom work, group processing, and personal supervision by a certified supervisor. Most seminaries offer academic credit toward the Master of Divinity degree for CPE training.

CPE training is offered in units or quarters. Generally speaking, one unit involves 400 hours of training offered in three months, but some centers offer part-time extended units. CPE is a challenging experience for most candidates, as it challenges the trainees personally and professionally. Tuition is required for the training; however, most centers providing one-year programs offer a stipend to cover the cost and at least some of the living expenses. Normally, year-long programs are offered to individuals who have at least one basic unit completed. The Canadian Association of Pastoral Practice and Education (CAPPE) is the Canadian counterpart of ACPE.

Professional certification is also an important part of preparation for institutional ministry. The most prominent professional organization in America is the Association of Professional Chaplains (APC), formerly the College of Chaplains. A seminary degree and CPE training qualify candidates to become members of the APC. Members who have four units of CPE and one year of experience in chaplaincy can apply for certification as Board Certified Chaplains (BCC).

Official credentials alone do not guarantee effective, Spirit-filled, institutional ministry. Credentials may open the door to a ministry position, but personal competence will prosper an individual in that position. Good chaplains must possess intrapersonal and interpersonal competences. Intrapersonal skills require a strong sense of personal identity; this includes an awareness of one's own strengths and weaknesses as a person and minister. A chaplain should also have an awareness of his or her own dynamics, as well as an understanding of his or her needs for personal growth. An effective institutional minister should be an integrated person, as personal wholeness is an important ingredient of success in institutional ministry. This type of minister can also affirm him- or herself. When ministry exists outside the walls of the church, no immediate community of faith is available to offer affirmation. The minister who is unable to affirm him- or herself in a wholesome way will find the work very difficult.

In the area of interpersonal relationships, an institutional minister needs the skills to work in a multireligious community, without losing his or her convictions or spiritual gifts. Individuals who are able to effectively communicate within their professional contexts do well in this ministry. A Spirit-filled minister, working in a multicultural context, must possess much wisdom in today's world. Christian ministry is not value neutral; an individual should not give up his or her values to work in a non-Christian environment. On the other hand, he or she will encounter much resistance and hostility if he or she employs only confrontational strategies. Recall that many saints worked in Caesar's palace during Saint Paul's time. One can work with others and still minister effectively, as the Lord opens the door for such ministry.

An effective institutional minister must be able to initiate, maintain, and appropriately terminate relationships with others. The minister should effectively utilize personal and ministerial authority in his relationships. An increasing number of Charismatic ministers are entering institutional service. Most of them are successful in their ministries; however, some who cannot make the contextual adjustment find it difficult to stay in this work. Institutional ministry is in need of more workers. I would like to encourage everyone who has a sense of calling to this ministry to pursue the required professional preparation.

Praise and Worship Ministry

I am always very pleased to see the involvement of young people in the life of the church. I have often encouraged church leaders to involve young people in the various ministries of their churches.

Providing leadership for praise and worship seems to be the area in which young people are most frequently involved. New life has emerged in many churches through the influence of young people, who bring more contemporary tunes into the services. I am concerned, however, over certain tendencies that have emerged in the youth-led music ministry in Charismatic churches. I believe the following fifteen suggestions would help praise and worship leaders improve the effectiveness of their ministry.

1. **Check Your Calling.** It is wise to confirm that you are called to the ministry of leading praise and worship. Do you have talent? Do people seem to sense God's presence when you lead them in worship? Do you consider your talents a gift from God, and do you desire to use them to glorify God and bless people? Enter into this ministry only after you have confirmed these issues within yourself. Don't assume you are called to music ministry just because someone else is doing it, or because you can play an instrument.
2. **Check Your Life.** If you are not living a sanctified life by the grace of God, it is better to voluntarily get off the stage. Worship led by an individual involved in unconfessed sin does not please God. Your testimony and credibility are a major part of your ministry. Before you approach the pulpit to minister to others, repent of your sins and be reconciled, as far as possible, with all people.
3. **Choose Songs Prayerfully.** Not all good songs are suitable for all occasions; the selected song must be appropriate for the ministerial occasion. Consider your purpose. Do you wish to lead people to praise God? Are you giving people an opportunity to dedicate themselves to God at the end of a service? Choose songs that are appropriate for the occasion and fitting to the specific portion of the service.

4. **Be Under Authority**. Do not take over the service in order to lead where you want to go. Always inquire about the goals of the service from the person who is in charge and identify how you can help reach those goals. Learn the order of service and discover its theme, so your music ministry will reinforce the major theme of the service.

5. **Watch Your Appearance and Body Movements**. Leading praise and worship is a ministry, not a performance; dress modestly and decently. While the rhythm of music influences the movement of one's physical body, a Christian minister's physical movements should be appropriate; your movements and appearance should not distract people from worship. As much as possible, be culturally appropriate to the congregation; avoid being perceived as a worldly person by the people in your context. Remember that worldly is defined differently by different cultures. Avoid all appearance of evil.

6. **Draw Attention to Jesus, Not Self**. Do not yield to the temptation to show off your talent in a way that draws attention to yourself rather than to God. Give your best, but don't cause people to focus their attention on your gifts and talents; keep your ego in check. Lead people to the throne of God, and let them see Jesus. You must decrease and Jesus must increase. People know talent when they see it, and they will appreciate you when they know you consider your talent a gift from God. This does not translate into putting yourself down. Humility is not denying the gift God has given you; rather, it is giving God the glory for the gift you have. Do not promote yourself over God.

7. **Promote the Word**. Some worship leaders drown the words of songs in loud music. Keep in mind that we worship with hymns, psalms, and spiritual songs; the words are important. Let the music serve the Word, not the other way around. Since

faith comes by hearing and hearing by the Word of God, allow the Word to prevail.

8. **Minimize Your Own Words.** Some music ministers talk too much between songs. If your calling is to preach, seek training and enter into a preaching ministry; do not camouflage yourself as a praise and worship leader and hold up the worship services. Lead the congregation to sing and glorify God with few words, and focus on leading worship.

9. **Respect Time.** Find out before the service how much time has been set aside for praise and worship and stay as close to the guideline as possible. When God is doing something in the midst of His people, it can be difficult to stop. Seek permission to continue at such times. Most service leaders will be sensitive to this; however, do not go against the presiding person and take over the service.

10. **Acknowledge Your Team.** Do not try to be a superstar and take all the glory if your team does well. God uses each musician differently, so acknowledge the contribution of your team members. Ministry is not a one person show.

11. **Listen to the Message and the Altar Call Carefully.** The concluding songs should flow with the message that was preached. If there was an altar call, the music should support it. The songs should also respect the mood of the service. Change or add to preplanned songs appropriately, if your team can handle it, and make smooth transitions.

12. **Motivate, Rather than Manipulate.** Music is a powerful vehicle, which can be used to motivate as well as manipulate. Be led by the Spirit and do not try to manipulate people. You cannot create a revival. Flow with the Spirit and allow the Lord to move by getting out of His way.

13. **Avoid Tampering with the Loudspeaker.** Prepare the speaker system for your needs before the service begins, as much as

possible. Tampering with the sound system and instruments for a lengthy period of time, in the middle of a service, is very distracting to the worshipers.

14. **Let God's People Sit**. If a lengthy song service is planned, please allow the congregation to be seated during part of that time. At least give permission to those who wish to sit down, so that they will not feel that they are dishonoring you and God by being seated. Most services have older or handicapped persons who are unable to stand up for a lengthy period of time. Remember that people stand up by themselves when God moves.

15. **Remember Uzzah**. Second Samuel 6 tells of a man named Uzzah, who touched the ark of the covenant. Though his intentions were good he died because he was forbidden by the Law to touch the ark. This happened while David, the great psalmist, led worship. Ministry may seem like something anyone can do. In some circles, the person with the loudest voice and most aggressive personality is the minister. This is not the biblical pattern. Ministry is a calling, and it must be performed humbly. Even in the New Testament, the sacred is guarded, and we are called to holiness and humility. Paul says that unworthiness causes many to "sleep" or to die; therefore, we must handle ministry with joyful devotion and grateful humility. Leading praise and worship is a great ministry; it should not be taken lightly. Lead with skill and enthusiasm, as well as with humility and joy. Then watch heaven open.

Continuing Education of Ministers

Well-meaning individuals often exhort ministry candidates using the words of the apostle Paul, "Study to shew thyself approved ..." (2 Tim. 2:15 KJV). Unfortunately, the exhorters seem to forget that these words were written to someone who was already in ministry. The apostle's words have more to do with the continuing development of a minister than with his or her preordination studies.

The church in America has always been concerned about the training of clergy. Historically, however, the attention of theological educators has been focused on the formal education of ministry candidates. Today the focus expands to include ministerial continuing education. Competence in ministry requires the continuing education of ministers.

Why Continuing Education?

Professionals are responding in different ways to today's changing society and the ongoing information explosion. A common response involves development and implementation of continuing education programs for practitioners. Ministry cannot afford to ignore this issue. Most clergy are practicing their profession in a world that is much different from that in which they were trained. They are forced to gain additional knowledge and skills to minister more effectively to persons traveling on the information superhighway. It is high time for all churches and denominations to require and fund ministerial lifelong education.

Unfortunately, it appears that ministers are tempted to take a fast-food approach to continuing education rather than a planned meal approach. Ministers would be better off assessing their own learning needs and intentionally planning to meet those needs. Fortunately, many learning resources are available today to meet the felt needs of the clergy.

History

According to Robert T. Frerichs, the modern movement of continuing education for ministry can trace its roots to the late nineteenth and early twentieth centuries.[8] For instance, historical evidence indicates that clergy gathered together on the frontier for the purpose of studying biblical exposition, polemics, practical theology, and elocution.

The Chautauqua movement, which began as a Sunday school movement and later became an adult education movement, had a tremendous impact on continuing the education of clergy in the early part of the twentieth century. Later, the land-grant universities played a vital role in the development of clerical continuing education. Eventually theological seminaries and denominations began to provide seminars, schools, and refresher courses.

The 1930s witnessed the founding of many clinical pastoral training programs. In the fifties and sixties, several organizations were born that influenced the continuing education of protestant ministers. Among these were The Interpreter's House at Lake Junaluska, founded by Carlyle Marney; the Pastoral Institute of Washington; the Institute of Advanced Pastoral Studies, founded by Reuel Howe at Bloomfield Hills in Michigan; the Society for the Advancement of Continuing Education in Ministry (SACEM); and the Academy of Parish Clergy.

The most notable development in the late twentieth century was the development and explosive growth of Doctor of Ministry degree programs. Studies have shown that status enhancement and aspirations for upward mobility are not the primary or decisive motives of most D.Min. students; rather, they are motivated by their continuing education needs. The Doctor of Ministry provides the opportunity to receive continuing education while pursuing a formal professional doctorate.

Needs

Careful studies of the continuing education needs of ministers have been conducted among clergy of different cities, regions, and denominations. According to James Berkley, ministers generally need remedial, retooling, and renewing education.[9] Connolly C. Gamble Jr. identifies needs according to the following categories: knowledge, growth, skills training, support systems, and therapy.[10]

Charles B. Fortier reports the following facts resulting from a study he conducted: (1) practically all of the clergy assessed expressed a great need for continuing education in relation to their various professional roles; (2) the practical areas of administration, public relations, and communication skills seemed to be of great interest; (3) clergy need to increase their competence in relation to counseling, race relations, drug problems, adolescent development, administration, and Christian education.[11]

Donald Emler studied the continuing education needs of clergy in relation to their midcareer development.[12] He looked specifically at United Methodist ministers, focusing on the continuing education needs of clergy based on their functional roles. The following educational needs were identified by midcareer ministers: improvement in communication skills; educational ministry skills; counseling skills; basic administration skills, such as multiple staff relations; and organizational development skills, such as planned change strategies. The study also identified understanding current trends in theological development as a need for ministers who had finished seminary training at least fifteen years earlier.

Jimmy Ward Walker prioritized the following continuing education needs of clergy, based on a study of the relationship between pastoral tenure and continuing education among Southern Baptist ministers: counseling, leadership, organizational development, church growth, evangelism, personal spiritual development, theological issues, personal development, social issues, preaching/communication, teaching, relational skills, and personal ministry.[13] Although the relationship between pastoral tenure and continuing education was insignificant, his study showed that a pastor's formal education was a major determining factor of his or her commitment to lifelong learning.

Other studies have identified the following additional needs for ministers: skill in group dynamics, theological development, combined lay-clergy educational experiences, self-acceptance, social action skills, conflict resolution skills, and enabling of others.

In a national survey of interdenominational chaplains which I conducted in 1992, I identified forty learning needs in three major areas: (1) professional skills, (2) knowledge, and (3) personal development. The highest rated needs in the professional skills area were: counseling, conflict resolution, and spiritual direction. The three top knowledge needs were: ethical issues, current theological issues, and spiritual development. The following were at the top of personal development needs: spiritual renewal, financial management, retirement planning, and self-care.[14]

Resources

The Doctor of Ministry degree program is a major resource for ministers with professional qualifications; it is now available in seminaries across North America. A great number of clergy are not able or willing to pursue a doctoral degree to meet their continuing education needs, despite the popularity of the D.Min. program. Fortunately, seminaries and Bible colleges do offer several types of nondegree continuing education programs.

Clinical Pastoral Education (CPE) is a widely used resource for the continuing education of clergy. CPE involves a structured educational process designed to increase pastoral effectiveness in counseling, pastoral care, and mental health ministries. Today, CPE training is available in hospitals, parishes, campuses, and correctional and geriatric facilities, as well as in seminaries.

Self-initiated projects present another avenue of learning for clergy. These not only include personal use of books, journals, magazines, and audio or video materials, but also meetings with colleagues for the purpose of learning from one another. According to one published report, thirteen ministers from Louisville, Kentucky, met periodically to help each other become better preachers. Their preaching seminar was self-initiated and cost effective. It began when one concerned minister reached out to his colleagues in the area.

Private and public universities continue to be great resources for ministers. Courses in counseling, communication, administration, and religious studies are available at these institutions.

Professional associations for clergy are proven resources of continuing education. The Academy of Parish Clergy, the Association of Professional Chaplains (formerly the College of Chaplains), and the American Association of Pastoral Counselors constitute examples of associations that offer continuing education opportunities for ministers. Pastors' schools and leadership conferences sponsored by independent ministries, as well as various denominations, are also resources for ministers.

Undergraduate and graduate degree programs are now available for clergy in modular and distance education formats in seminaries, Bible colleges, and universities. In addition to the traditional courses, various innovative delivery systems are now available. Charles Snow, an adult educator, lists the following systems: extension courses where instructors are transported to the external sites, establishment of extension centers with some permanent faculty, packaging courses in short-term modules so the student is on campus only for short periods of time, construction of independent directed-study courses, and fully online courses. Non-degree programs are also available through the non-traditional avenues.

High technology has opened up new continuing education resources for clergy. For example, Internet conferences and webinars are easily available on so many topics. Several educational conferences are simultaneously aimed at social workers, clergy, and other professionals. These explosive developments in high tech, communication, and the Internet have created more innovative means of lifelong education for the clergy.

Being Healthy in Ministry

Ministry presents many challenges that can cause a person to burn out. For instance, a minister is constantly dealing with people in need, and the work may seem repetitious. It is also hard to know if the hard work is being effective. Being mindful of these and other challenges and having healthy ways to cope with them will help one prevent burnout. Practicing self-care, having a good support system, and being able to celebrate small successes will assist a minister. Burnout normally results from giving out more than one is receiving. In that sense, a minister who is able to receive spiritual nourishment on an ongoing basis will be able to give out without getting burned out.

There are healthy and sick ways of functioning in ministry. A competent minister must try to remain healthy in ministry. Paul Pruyser's *The Minister as Diagnostician* has been helpful in my endeavor to define a healthy person. In view of the fact that ministry is about making people whole, a minister of the gospel must also walk in wholeness. Pruyser presents certain theological themes that are useful for ministers in their work of diagnosing the needs of people. I have found that these same themes reflect the characteristics of healthy persons.

One assumes that a healthy person is born again and baptized in the Holy Spirit. One should also assume that the individual maintains a wholesome Christian lifestyle or a sanctified life. I believe that Pruyser's themes add to these basic characteristics of a healthy person. Pruyser's themes as I understand them in this context are briefly described below:

1) *Awareness of the holy.* A healthy person must be aware of the presence of a holy God in his or her life. People often describe their life issues in such a way that one wonders where God is in respect to their situation. An individual's awareness of the presence of God in his or her life is a sign of health.

2) *Sense of providence.* Providence is a theological term that means that God the Creator takes care of His creation. A healthy person is one who has an assurance that God will meet his or her needs, so that he or she can face the challenges and issues of life from a position of confidence. God's providence covers His entire creation. A sense of providence enables an individual to live by faith, in the knowledge that God will supply all his or her needs through Christ Jesus (Phil. 4:19).

3) *Stance of faith.* Someone has said that faith sees the invisible, believes the incredible, and accomplishes the impossible. According to the writer of Hebrews, faith is the substance of things hoped for and the evidence of things not seen. A healthy person is one who looks at his or her world through the eyes of faith. Just as eyeglasses affect a person's vision, faith affects a person's view of life. A healthy person is one who walks by faith and not by sight alone. Faith enables an individual to believe in God's providence; faith believes that God is faithful. When we consider all the "by faith" statements in Hebrews chapter 11, it becomes clear that the author is describing life as an adventure of faith. A healthy person must have this type of faith.

4) *Experience of gratefulness.* A healthy person lives a thankful life in which his or her attitude is based on gratitude. Unfortunately, gratefulness is a rare commodity in an affluent society. A healthy person enjoys God's grace with gratitude. Gratitude does not depend on the size of the gift; it flows out of one's relationship with the giver.

5) *Process of repenting.* All born-again Christians believe that God has forgiven their sins. The Christian life is a forgiven life. All of us, however, are subject to sins of commission and omission. This means that we must live with an attitude of repentance. The ability to experience *metanoia* (repentance), to ask for forgiveness, and to live in humility are evidences of a spiritually wholesome life.

6) *Feeling of communion.* A sense of community fosters communion. A healthy Christian experiences communion with God and with the members of the community of faith. This extends beyond the sacrament of communion, to a sense of belonging and intimacy. A healthy person has the capacity for intimacy with God and humankind. All

of us have met long-term members of a particular church who describe the church as "their" (other people's) church. Regardless of the cause, this attitude reflects the absence of a sense of communion with the body of Christ. Having a sense of belonging and community is a sign of health and wholeness.

7) *Sense of vocation.* Ministry is a vocation, which stems from a calling. In Christian life, all are called by God; therefore, all Christians must see their life's work, whatever that might be, as a vocation. Both plumbers and preachers ought to live their Christian lives as vocations, but for ministers this attitude is an absolute necessity. A healthy person is one who sees his or her life's work as a vocation.

Pruyser's themes are important clues to wholeness. Born-again, Spirit-filled, and sanctified persons who demonstrate these qualities are truly healthy children of God. Ministers will benefit from examining their own lives with respect to these diagnostic themes as they seek to develop a competent Spirit-empowered ministry.

Chapter 5

Preaching in the Power of the Spirit

> Preach the word; be prepared in season and out of season; correct, rebuke and encourage—with great patience and careful instruction.
> —2 Timothy 4:2

God made the decision to save the world through the "foolishness" of preaching. All Christians have been touched by this foolishness at some point in their lives; somewhere, someone, in some way preached Jesus, and that act impacted the listeners and brought many of them to a new way of life. Biblical preaching is still converting the world and confounding the wise.

There is a difference between the foolishness of preaching and foolish preaching. A lot of preaching today is simply foolish. There are lazy preachers who refuse to study and prepare to deliver the Word of God to the people of God in the power of the Holy Spirit. Extemporaneous, superficial preaching hurts the body of Christ. Many ministers seem to have time for everything but study. As a theological educator, this is a matter of great concern to me.

The New Testament strongly testifies to the importance of preaching as a chief component of Christian ministry. Notice the following passages:

> What then shall we say, brothers? When you come together, everyone has a hymn, or a word of instruction, a revelation, a tongue or an interpretation. All of these must be done for the strengthening of the church (1 Cor. 14:26).

> Speak to one another with psalms, hymns and spiritual songs. Sing and make music in your heart to the Lord, always giving thanks to God the Father for everything, in the name of our Lord Jesus Christ (Eph. 5:19, 20).

> Let the word of Christ dwell in you richly as you teach and admonish one another with all wisdom, and as you sing psalms, hymns and spiritual songs with gratitude in your hearts to God (Col. 3:16).

> Preach the Word; be prepared in season and out of season; correct, rebuke and encourage—with great patience and careful instruction (2 Tim. 4:2).

The order of worship in the synagogues of the first century provides insight into the priority of preaching in the early church. As Christian believers left the synagogues for other places of worship, they took with them many aspects of Jewish worship. According to William Hendriksen, a typical order of synagogue worship followed a pattern of (1) thanksgiving, (2) responsive "Amen," (3) reading of a passage from the Pentateuch, (4) reading from the prophets, (5) a sermon or word of exhortation, and (6) benediction by a priest or a closing prayer by someone else in the absence of a priest.[1] According to William Willimon, the words of Luke 4:16–21, as well as early church history, confirm this outline.[2]

A public service described in Nehemiah 8:8 gives the outline of preaching in the Old Testament: "They read from the Book of the Law of God, making it clear and giving the meaning so that the people could understand what was being read." It appears that reading, translation, and explanation were involved in this exercise. Other scholars, such as Aldwin Ragoonath, believe that Old Testament preaching had three parts: reading, translation, and explanation with application.[3] The purpose of preaching was to make the Law clear to the people; increasing their understanding for the purpose of obedience was the deeper goal. New Testament preaching pursued the same purpose, with a new law of grace.

Several types of preaching exist. According to Ralph G. Turnbull, preaching can be categorized into twenty-five different types, including topical, situational, psychological, dispensational, missionary, ethnic, and others.[4] The most commonly used sermons can be categorized as topical, textual, or expository.

Historically, the prophetic preaching of the Old Testament was the first type of preaching identified. Modern textual/expository preaching evolved in the synagogue movement, which began during the captivity of Israel. It is clear that Jesus approved of such preaching. He attended synagogue worship, not only in Jerusalem, but also at other locations (Luke 4:16–21; Matt. 9:35; Mark 1:21). According to Luke, synagogue attendance was His custom (Luke 4:16).

Ragoonath provides a very helpful study of the New Testament words for preaching and teaching to support the idea that biblical preaching is essential. These words provide a composite definition of preaching.

KERUSSEIN = declaration, announce good news

EUANGELIZESTHAI = to proclaim good news, to declare gospel of salvation

MARTUREIN = witness (testifying personal experience)

DIDASKEIN = to teach, to deliver didactic discourse

PROPHETEUEIN = prophet

PARAKALEIN = exhorting

Gerhard Friedrich's definition of a prophet is relevant in this regard: "The prophet is the Spirit-endowed counselor of the community who tells us what to do in a specific situation; who blames and praises, whose preaching contains admonition and comfort, the call for repentance and promise."[5] The apostle Paul describes a prophet as an individual who offers exhortation, edification, and comfort (1 Cor. 14:3). As such, Paul's description supports the idea of preaching as a prophetic act in the New Testament.

According to Ragoonath, a good sermon possesses the following qualities:

1. It is biblical. A good sermon must be based on the Word of God.
2. It applies clearly to people's situations and needs. Effective preaching addresses the needs of the listeners.
3. It results from reflective thinking. Superficial preaching does not impact congregations. Reflective thinking provides deeper insights.
4. It is pastoral. Sermons must reveal a shepherd's heart.

5. It is positive. Even unpleasant issues can be dealt with in a positive manner.
6. It is delivered naturally. A good preacher is true to his or her own personality and natural attributes such as voice, gestures, and so forth.

Eight Preaching Principles

Ragoonath also posits the following eight crucial principles for sound preaching:

1. Highest view of scripture: The preacher must perceive the Bible as the inspired Word of God.
2. Adequate preparation: The preacher must do his or her homework.
3. Textual and expository: The sermon must be biblical.
4. Homiletical order: The sermon needs logical order that should be derived from the text.
5. Relevant: The message must be relevant to the situation and needs of the listener.
6. Christocentric: Jesus Christ must be the center of the message.
7. Evangelistic: The message must share the good news.
8. Pastoral in nature: The message should be given from a shepherd's heart.[6]

It is important for preachers to consider these principles in the preparation and evaluation of sermons.

Gijsbert D. J. Dingemans maintains that preaching should have three levels:

1. A level of explanation, information, and clarification for teaching.

2. A level of proclamation, persuasion, and appeal to transmit the power of the text to move and confront.
3. A level of basic trust and interrelationship in order to show the credibility of the text, church, and the preacher for consolidation and confirmation of common faith.[7]

Spirit-filled preachers must take into account the tremendous cultural challenge that all Christian preachers face in the twenty-first century: Modern America embraces a certain type of religious pluralism that basically believes that all gods are equal. The best of Christianity has always shown respect for other religions, but present society demands a level of acceptance and endorsement over and above respect. One cannot endorse all religions as viable spiritual paths and simultaneously declare the uniqueness of Jesus Christ. The task of overcoming societal challenges in order to preach the gospel will be an ongoing issue for all evangelicals in North America, but particularly for Pentecostals and Charismatics who are committed to a Spirit-empowered perspective on preaching.

Charles Snow, former professor of preaching and leadership at Oral Roberts University School of Theology and Ministry, outlined some of the challenges faced by biblical preachers in this century. He believes that biblical communicators must find new and creative ways to share the life-giving message of the gospel with today's digital generation. Snow considers Bill Easum's assessment of the current culture relevant. Easum makes several observations:

1. North America is now one of the prime mission fields in the world.
2. Many forms of truth are replacing ultimate truth.
3. The twentieth century emphasis on property and the importance of place is being replaced by an emphasis on relationship and community.

4. The Digital Age has already replaced the Information Age.
5. People are moving to the cities, and boats are no longer coming from Europe. The new immigrants are coming from Hispanic and Asian cultures.
6. Biogenetics is beginning to rearrange our understanding of human actions to the extent that we will soon be able to attribute anything to "my genes made me do it."[8]

Rick Warren agrees with Easum:

1. Proclaimers of truth do not get much attention in a society that devalues truth.
2. The majority of Americans reject the idea of absolute truth.
3. They value tolerance more than truth.
4. Moral relativism is at the root of what is wrong in our society.[9]

Preachers must decide that regardless of popular opinion, they must continue to preach the good news and declare the truth of the gospel. Christianity has often preached to a hostile world. America is forced to learn from this heritage, believing that somehow the foolishness of preaching still works because the totality of preaching is much more than what the preacher says and does.

In any case, preachers must recognize the following observations made by Tim Timmons and respond appropriately:

1. The world is looking for quick-fix answers.
2. The church has gotten used to talking to itself.
3. The sermon and worship experiences are directed at those who own the church.[10]

Trevor Grizzle, professor of New Testament at Oral Roberts University Seminary, defined New Testament preaching as evangelistic in intent as it unfolds and applies the implications of the gospel to lead the believer into greater discipleship and maturity in Christ. Grizzle stated, "New Testament preaching is more evangelistic, more democratized (Acts 8:4), Christ-centered, and is attended often by the miraculous." According to Grizzle, the Old Testament prophets were forerunners of the New Testament heralds. Their messages were always "practical, pointed and vivid."

Grizzle described the preacher as God's ambassador (2 Cor. 5:20; Eph. 6:20), a medium of God's power, and a megaphone of God's voice (Acts 2:14). A preacher has a sense of oughtness and urgency (Mark 1:38; Acts 4:20; 1 Cor. 9:16), and he or she is a transparent person who adapts his or her presentation to his or her audience (Acts 14, 17, 22). According to Grizzle, the content of New Testament preaching includes the following:

1. The good news about the kingdom of God and the Name of Jesus (Acts 8:12).
2. The death, resurrection, and exaltation of Jesus (Acts 2:23–24).
3. The Lordship of Jesus (Acts 2:36).
4. A summons to repent and receive forgiveness (Acts 2:38, 3:19, 5:31, 10:43).
5. Christ's return (Acts 3:21).

Grizzle listed nine essentials of New Testament preaching:

1. Christ-centered
2. Spirit-empowered
3. Simple and practical
4. Contemporized biblical saving acts of God

5. Adapted to the audience
6. Attended by the miraculous
7. Demands response and offers hope
8. Bold confidence in call, calling, and message
9. Targeted and purposeful

Biblical preaching is, by nature, goal-oriented; preachers do their work for a response. Lawrence Lacour, former professor of preaching at Oral Roberts University Seminary, asked his students: "Why preach if you don't expect a response? Why preach if there is no call to respond?" In an unorthodox way, Lacour compared preaching to selling cars. "Why do you go through the whole sales process if you have no plans to make people sign on the dotted line at the end?" he asked. We must keep in mind that there are at least three reasons for preaching, Lacour said: to give information, to convince or persuade, and to motivate action.

Biblical preaching has homiletical order; the text supplies the logic of the message. According to Ragoonath, one can discover this logic by finding the Holy Spirit's intent in the text. "The preacher must be a logician and a rhetorician," said Luther.[11] This does not mean, however, that preaching is just a commentary on the text. Martyn Lloyd-Jones said, "Preaching is not a running commentary. It has form, pattern and relevance."[12] The most important aspect of preaching is what God speaks to the people through the message. Zach Eswine makes this point in *Preaching to a Post-Everything World*. "God is the hero of every text," he says, and preaching must echo creation, fall, redemption and heaven.[13]

In *Preaching in the Spirit*, Dennis F. Kinlaw makes several constructive suggestions for modern preachers. He advises preachers to read well, emphasizing that the Bible should be our primary, but not exclusive, reading. Kinlaw recalls Oswald Chambers' words: "A man who reads only the Bible never really reads the Bible."[14] Good preaching can offend the hearers from time to time. One should not hesitate to preach on issues of the day as needed. John Wycliffe, for instance, preached against popes, confession to priests, and materialism in the church. According to Howard Ervin, one of my seminary professors, preaching must comfort the afflicted and afflict the comfortable. The preacher must remember that when it comes to evangelistic preaching, he or she is never the first witness in the hearer's life. The Holy Spirit is at work preparing the way long before the preacher arrives.

Good preaching is not just a matter of technique; the relationship of the preacher to the people is also a very important factor. The preparation of the preacher as a vessel of God is the most important aspect of Spirit-filled preaching. In preaching, the preacher offers that which he or she has first received. Kinlaw says that the preacher plays the role of a midwife; God reached the preacher through Jesus Christ, and Christ reaches the world through the preacher.

Spirit-empowered preaching is not just oration; it is an event. Something happens as the Word of God is preached. It takes place at the intersection of the preacher, the people, and the Word of God, and it happens through the intervention of the Holy Spirit. Pentecostal preaching is preaching in the power of the Holy Spirit. It is powerful preaching that transcends the preacher's personality and stamina.

Esteemed scholar David Buttrick says that preaching is phenomenological. He describes preaching as an event that forms faith consciousness in the individual and the community. Preaching is more than an explanation of the text or a discourse on psychological well-being; preaching forms a faith world in which the hearers may live and love. Buttrick says that revelation is not something that was just written or reported; it is something that happens currently. Revelation is not just out there or back in history, and preaching should not be reduced to an explanation of past events to a current congregation. Preaching must participate in God's ongoing redemptive purposes. This implies that preaching should leave open the possibility for biblical revelation to take place again, not to add to the Bible, but to comprehend it. To a certain extent, Buttrick seems to describe the preaching of the gospel with signs following, which is what Pentecostal/Charismatic preaching should be.

What is unique about Spirit-empowered preaching? It is the preaching of the gospel that is anointed by the Holy Spirit. It is preaching about Jesus in the power of the Holy Spirit. Spirit-empowered preaching involves the body, mind, spirit, and emotions of the preacher in the declaration of the Word of God under the inspiration of the Holy Spirit. Simply put, Spirit-empowered preaching is preaching by a person filled with the Holy Spirit.

Spirit-Led Interpretation of the Bible

Have you noticed the way a particular scripture verse is used to establish opposing theological positions? Whether it is about tithing or wearing ornaments, scripture verses are often interpreted in multiple ways. You may have noticed that different faith groups come to differing positions on the baptism of the Holy Spirit and speaking in tongues based on the very same biblical texts. What you are seeing is the difference in biblical interpretation. The text may be the same, but the ultimate impact of any text is based on the way it is interpreted.

There are correct and wrong ways of interpreting a biblical text. You may be surprised to know that some of the favorite theological beliefs among God-fearing Christians are based on irresponsible interpretations of biblical texts. Preachers and teachers of the Bible must take their work of interpretation very seriously because wrong interpretations leave to wrong doctrines, and wrong doctrines affect people's lives in this world and the next.

It appears that untrained preachers are not the only ones who interpret biblical texts in a biased way; pastors trained in Bible schools and seminaries seem to do the same based on their own or their school's particular orientation. Preaching based strictly on traditional ways of interpreting the Bible can impact Pentecostal and Charismatic congregations in very negative ways.

For instance, the main aim of Evangelical approaches to Bible interpretation is to find the historical meaning of particular texts. This is, of course, a very important goal. But what the text meant to someone in the original readership should not be the only concern of the Spirit-filled interpreter. What is the Holy Spirit saying through the same text to current believers should also be a concern for Spirit-filled interpreters because Pentecostals believe that the Spirit of God is actively at work in the world today, revealing God's word and ways to humankind, especially through His church. Why should they strictly adopt a method of interpreting the Bible that has led many to the conclusion that the gifts of the Holy Spirit have ceased operating?

Pentecostal interpreters of the Bible are not just passive readers. They are persons who are actively engaged in discovering the meaning of a particular passage by allowing the Spirit to move within them and interact between them and the text. The Spirit illuminates the Word, giving the interpreters not only important historical understanding, but also fresh insights and revelations! The readers and hearers of the Bible need more than the historical meaning of biblical passages; they also need to grasp the meaningfulness of the text in the now. Preaching without this element will be stale.

Early Pentecostal interpreters and preachers took the Bible as a dynamic document. They were not stuck on the historical meaning of what they read in the Bible; they considered the contexts of texts, but were also looking for the meaning of the texts in their own contexts. This is a valid way to interpret the Bible. The scripture does more than inform; it also transforms. Interpretation of biblical texts that is faithful to their historical contexts and illuminated by the Holy Spirit is what transforms lives profoundly. This may seem radical to some interpreters, but based on recent scholarship, Spirit-filled preachers must consider this perspective.[15] Even mainline preacher and Duke Divinity School preaching professor Richard Lischer has called ministers to go beyond the interpretive tradition of scientific criticism. He has asked interpreters to practice theological exegesis instead, which is "biblical interpretation that is sifted through the life, doctrines, and practices of the community for which it was intended and in which it is practiced."[16] He called on preachers to become religious readers of the Bible who must allow "the light of the text to illuminate his or her own life and that of the congregation."[17]

Studying the Bible should not only lead to knowing about God; it should also present opportunities to know God. Spirit-filled teachers, preachers, and other interpreters should be mindful of this. The Holy Spirit reveals God; preachers and other interpreters of a biblical text should ask, what is the Spirit saying to God's people through this text now?

Isn't this too subjective? Can't people misunderstand what the Spirit is saying? How would you prevent false doctrines from developing from personal interpretations and claims? These are good questions, but this is where the importance of the community of faith comes in. God has His Word, His Spirit, and His community to discern and guard the truth. It is the job of the Sprit-filled community to test the interpretation for authenticity and witness and to keep the doctrines in balance. What else should be inferred from the words of the apostle Peter, "It seemed good to the Holy Spirit and to us ..." (Acts 15:28)?

Chapter 6
Teaching As Jesus Taught

> He proclaimed the kingdom of God and taught about the Lord
> Jesus Christ—with all boldness and without hindrance!
> —Acts 28:31

Jesus was a master teacher. He preached the kingdom of God, manifested the power of the kingdom, and taught the mysteries of the kingdom to His disciples. Often the disciples asked Jesus privately for detailed explanations of the parables and issues He discussed in public. He revealed truth and explained mysteries to them that He did not share with the public. The Gospels describe many moments of learning and discovery among Jesus's disciples.

Teaching is a very important ministry. Today's church is in desperate need of well-trained teachers and Christian educators. The current generation's tendency to make short-term commitments has affected the church in the area of Christian education. It is unfortunate that some Charismatic churches do not have any intentional Christian education programs; in some circles the entire ministry of the church has boiled down to weekly celebrations!

Jesus called His disciples to preach, *teach*, and heal. The teaching ministry of the church must not be neglected. A church that does not teach is short-sighted, and it will have a difficult future. The church is called to make disciples of all nations by teaching them to obey everything Jesus has commanded (Matt. 28:20). This cannot be done without adequate planning, preparation, and commitment of resources.

Christians are commanded to "grow in the grace and knowledge of our Lord" (2 Pet. 3:18). Without a learning process, one cannot grow; yet it is unclear who is responsible to provide this opportunity in many congregations. Christian education should not be left to untrained volunteers; neither should it be the sole domain of church ladies. There should not be any doubt that the senior pastor of a church is responsible to ensure that adequate teaching and training opportunities exist in the church. A healthy church is a learning community, and all members of the community, including the pastors, must be learners. Christian life involves lifelong learning.

Churches of the new century are in need of a Bible-based, Holy Spirit-empowered teaching-learning process, which should involve all members of the faith community. When each member learns how to apprehend and obey God's purpose for his or her life in Jesus Christ, everyone will be able to serve effectively in some form of ministry. The ultimate purpose of such a program should be to make mature disciples who will be imitators of the Master Teacher, Jesus, in this generation.

Jesus, Teaching, and the Holy Spirit

Jesus must become the model teacher in the pulpit and the classroom. Several writers have identified Jesus's qualities as a teacher. Jesus, as a teacher, was a man of love, excitement, and optimism. He was an approachable teacher who believed in an informal way of teaching. Jesus taught as one with authority, yet with profound simplicity. Jesus emphasized the pupil, not Himself, and He always started with the student's needs. Jesus was not a boring teacher because He believed in using a variety of teaching methods, such as questions, discussions, lectures, and stories. He often incorporated everyday objects as teaching tools.

A good teacher must make room for the Holy Spirit to move in his or her classroom because the Spirit is the principal teacher who will lead everyone to truth. The ultimate truth is Jesus, who described Himself as the Way, the Truth, and the Life. The Holy Spirit helps both the teacher and the learners, and He prepares the environment for the proper transmission of truth. First, the Holy Spirit enables the teacher to understand the truth; then He opens the mind of the student to receive the truth. Without the assistance of the Holy Spirit, the impact of teaching is limited.

The purpose of teaching is not just the simple transfer of information; Christian education is transformational. Studying God's Word involves change and transformation. Instead of conforming to the world, God's people are called to be transformed by the renewing of their minds. This transformational process should be the basic outcome of teaching.

Educational Philosophy

Christian educators need an appropriate philosophy of education. Philosophy deals with reality, truth, and value. In the realm of reality, educators must deal with the nature of the learner and the role of the teacher; the area of truth deals with the curriculum; and the area of value addresses issues of ethics, helping to understand what is good and valuable.

In Christian education, the learner can be defined as one loved by God; he or she is someone for whom Jesus died on the cross. The role of the teacher is to teach, embody, and impart the truth that is taught; modeling is the best form of teaching.

The teaching curriculum is the Word of God; it is Truth with a capital T. For a Christian educator, the truth of God's Word is not negotiable; it is not truth with a small t. This is a difficult concept for twenty-first century people to fathom, because this generation takes pride in its faith in relativism, being so used to updating scientific truths that this generation has a difficult time believing in a truth that is established forever.

To define what is good, one needs to look to God and His Word; His plans and purposes are good. A good Christian educator is mindful of this. Before Oral Roberts University was founded, its founder shook the world with the simple statement, "God is a good God." He received much abuse for stating that basic truth from Psalm 118:1, because the culture could not handle it at that time. Oral Roberts University as a Christian educational enterprise was built on the idea that God is a good God and that He wants to bless His creation!

A Christian educator should not approach people of other faiths with contempt. Stanley Jones, the great missionary statesman who devoted his life to teaching the Hindus of India about Christ, taught and modeled this lesson. Christians do not need to profane the names of other gods in order to share their faith in Jesus Christ. Releasing the floodlight called Jesus Christ does not translate into cursing the darkness around; accept people as they are and love them where they are; then, like Paul at Athens, introduce the truth of the gospel in a way that these people can understand. The goal of Christian education is not to colonize the world; rather, it is to share the love of God that is shed abroad in the teachers' hearts. Christian educators must seek to release the light of Jesus into the dark corners of our world. They must share the life they have discovered in Jesus with others, for they live, move, and have their being in Him. Teaching is a life-giving ministry.

Good Teaching

Teaching must rely on more than the brain of the student in order to be effective. According to Larry Richards, good teaching must involve understanding, emotions, values, and decisions on the part of the teacher.[1] It takes patience, presence, and persistence to be a good teacher of God's Word. Patience allows a teacher to lovingly accept the student, and presence represents availability without invasion; persistence means presenting God's truth faithfully. Thus, teaching is more than just talking or letting the students talk. It must extend beyond the classroom or the sanctuary and incorporate planning, inspiring, caring, and modeling.

Teachers should also consider their students' ability to retain information. It is estimated that students retain only 10 percent of what they hear and 30 percent of what they see, but they will retain 90 percent of what they hear, see, say, and practice.[2]

If this is the case, pastors and teachers need to do more than talk. Leonard Sweet, in *Postmodern Pilgrims*, calls students in the postmodern world the EPIC generation: (1) experiential, (2) participative, (3) image-based and (4) connected (online).[3] This means that teachers need to incorporate new methods to enhance learning, such as video, PowerPoint, drama, storytelling, and dialogue, in addition to discussion, debate, and group exercises. Stated more technically, learning involves three domains within the student: the affective, the cognitive, and the behavioral (psycho-motor). The *affective* realm primarily involves feelings and emotions; in this area a teacher should aim to create inspiration in the student. The *cognitive* domain involves students' knowledge and intellect. Students will grow in this area to the degree that the teaching content is effective. The *behavioral* area of learning impacts the will and the activities of the student, and will be reflected in his or her lifestyle.

The twenty-first century has ushered in a culture of entertainment, reverse values, violence, and materialism. Christians are called to communicate the gospel to such a culture. In order to meet this challenge, educators need to do more than just pursue business as usual. Pastors and teachers must acquire an adequate understanding of how people of all ages learn and then apply that understanding to their teaching ministry. Competent teachers are needed to teach children and adults.

Adult Education

The last part of the twentieth century witnessed the growth of the field known as adult education. Malcolm S. Knowles is considered the father of the adult education movement. Known as *andragogy* (learning of adults), as opposed to *pedagogy* (learning of children), this field studies adult learners.[4] Although it can be said that good pedagogy techniques would also be effective as andragogy, there are some unique aspects of adult education that do not fully apply to children. For instance, Knowles suggests that there are five assumptions of adult education that should be taken seriously by teachers of adults. These assumptions involve (1) concept of the learner (as self-directed), (2) role of the learner's experience (as rich resource), (3) readiness to learn (based on demands of life), (4) orientation to learning (problem-centered or solution oriented), and (5) motivation (based on internal incentives or curiosity).[5]

By considering Knowles' perspective, pastors will be able to avoid teaching adults as if they were children. A teacher is more than an individual who provides information; he or she must become a guide and mentor to the adult students.

The sole purpose of some teachers is to enable students to commit information to rote memory. A teacher who instructs and tests based on this goal, only measures the student's ability to memorize. Although it is a good thing to memorize the Word of God, according to Benjamin Bloom, memorization is the lowest level of cognitive activity. Bloom lists six levels of intellectual learning, ranging from the lowest to the highest:

1. Knowledge: student is able to recall.
2. Comprehension: student is able to explain the information.
3. Application: student can use the information in a meaningful way.
4. Analysis: student can see the relationship between concepts.
5. Synthesis: student is able to combine ideas and see the bigger picture.
6. Evaluation: student is able to make informed judgment.[6]

According to Raymond Wlodkowski, an effective teacher of adults is a good facilitator, who exhibits the following four characteristics. First, he or she will have *expertise* in the field of teaching. For example, a Bible teacher must have a good knowledge of the Word of God. Secondly, a good facilitator has *empathy* toward the student. Empathy helps the teacher present the material with a special concern for the learner's needs. A good facilitator is *enthusiastic* about the student, the subject, and the teaching-learning process. Finally, according to Wlodkowski, a good facilitator possesses *clarity* of thought and presentation.[7]

An effective facilitator also models what he or she teaches and acts as an expert resource person who knows the subject area well. He or she must be a good counselor who is interested in the learner's academic as well as nonacademic life and can act as a guide for the learning process using a variety of teaching methods.

Ultimately, a good teacher wants to move the adult student from a dependent learner to a self-directed learner. This requires the teacher to frequently change his or her role from coach to salesman, to facilitator, and to consultant. The Foundation for Critical Thinking presents the following tactics for promoting active learning:

1. Have the student summarize what has been taught in his or her own words.
2. Elaborate on what has been said.
3. Relate the issue being discussed to the student's own life experience.
4. Give examples to clarify and support what is said.
5. Show connection between related concepts.
6. Let the student state the question at issue.
7. Let the student restate instructions in his or her own words.
8. Describe to what extent his or her current point of view is similar or different from the teachers' or others'.
9. Put a response into written form.
10. Write down the most pressing question on the student's mind.
11. Discuss any of the above with a partner.

It appears that adults learn best when teachers use methods that:

1. Reduce anxiety.
2. Let the student show what he or she knows.

3. Give clear directions.
4. Show the relevance of the lesson.
5. Value the accuracy of responses or activities over the speed of response.
6. Repeat the information and allow deep processing.
7. Pace the lesson presentation at a reasonable speed.
8. Avoid distractions and interference.
9. Give both visual and auditory stimuli.
10. Make sure that the student is physically comfortable in the classroom.[8]

The teaching ministry of the church has not matched the challenges of the postmodern world. Postmodern society imposes so many major issues on individuals that they clearly require more resources than the ability to quote a verse or two. Individuals must be taught to make decisions and abide by them as kingdom citizens in this world. In this way believers can develop the capacity to make internal decisions about their lifestyles.

Teaching Teens

Some time ago, I conducted a training seminar for Sunday school teachers of teens in New York City. Teachers and leaders from more than thirty-five churches in New York City gathered in one place for this teachers' training event. Sponsored by the regional leaders of a Sunday school association, the sessions were attended by men and women from all walks of life who teach adolescents in churches.

After conversing with pastors and teachers at this seminar, I became convinced that teacher training, particularly for those teaching teens, is a tremendous need. Often the teachers recruited for these classes are untrained volunteers or people who do not feel a calling to teach teens. This is a grave mistake. Christian education is serious work that is to be conducted with concern and competence.

The world's information generation requires specially trained teachers. Today's teens do not live in the world in which many of their teachers were educated and the instruction they receive in their secular schools with cutting-edge technology is much different from what their teachers experienced as students. They will not respond well to a business-as-usual-type low budget Sunday school.

Consider, again, the fact that teenagers today are a generation that has access to information without supervision. Previously, young people went to teachers, authority figures, and experts for information. Teachers still need to present information, but much information is available to the students before they meet the teacher. Modern teaching must take this reality into account.

Once upon a time, teaching was conceptualized as pouring information from the teacher, the big bucket, into the pupil, the little bucket. This pedagogical model is now outdated. Teachers need to provide more than information; students must also be taught how to use the information, especially by developing the capability to evaluate the information for truthfulness and faithfulness to the Word of God.

Information sharing should not be the only purpose of Sunday schools; transformation of individuals through discipleship should be the ultimate goal. This requires caring teachers who have a call on their lives and who are willing to train themselves in modern teaching methods that take into account the true nature of today's learners.

A discussion on effective Christian education must begin with two questions. First, what is Christian education? Secondly, what is the purpose of Christian education? Christian education is a Bible-based, Holy Spirit-empowered, Christ-centered, and mission-driven teaching-learning process. The purpose of Christian education is to guide individuals at all stages of life through contemporary teaching methodologies to help them grow in grace and the knowledge of the Lord Jesus Christ and to equip them for effective ministry.

Christian education's ultimate purpose is to produce transformed lives. This transformation does not happen accidentally; it requires a strategy. The teacher should model Jesus Christ, the master educator, and follow His directive to make disciples. Jesus the Master Teacher always emphasized the pupil. He was a teacher of great authority and profound simplicity. He taught with definite goals and always started with the pupils' needs.

Jesus used a variety of teaching methods, such as questions, discussions, lectures, stories, and teaching aids. There is a need to think creatively to find contemporary applications of Jesus's methods of teaching.

Teaching teenagers necessitates that the teacher understand their physical, mental, social, and spiritual characteristics. Physically, teens deal with bursts of energy and recurring fatigue because they grow and develop at a rapid pace. They feel awkward about their bodies and their disproportionate growth. Teenagers also have keen minds and are often critical of everyone and everything as they begin to evaluate truth about the world for themselves. Teens experience mood swings and are given to daydreaming. Socially, they are greatly influenced by their peers, with a particular awareness of the opposite sex, whom they try to impress. They are in the process of transferring loyalty from their parents to peers. Although they may act otherwise, teens especially need acceptance from teachers, who are very important to them. Teens generally look to younger adults as role models. They are also sincere and serious about their spiritual life; they possess a desire to know God, but need guidance. Teenagers cannot handle long boring lectures; rather, they prefer learning activities that will enhance their spiritual development through social interactions. The following is a short list of activities in which teens would enthusiastically involve themselves.

Possible Activities/Methods for Teens

Word Puzzles
Mime
Skits
Role Playing
Interviews
Debates
Brainstorming
Buzz Groups
Panel Discussions
Paraphrasing Class Discussion
Creating News Stories
Writing Parables
Music

Teaching for Daily Decisions

Although Christian conversion is an internal matter, the Christian life displays external evidence. The New Testament documents biographies of individuals whose lives were transformed by an encounter with Jesus. The Samaritan woman who met Jesus at the well was changed by that encounter (John 4:39), and the demoniac who met Jesus received a sound mind (Luke 8:35). Similarly, the despised tax collector Zacchaeus became a philanthropist as he met Jesus in Jericho (Luke 19:8). The story of the Ethiopian eunuch testifies that an encounter with Jesus through the mediation of an evangelist is as powerful as an encounter with Jesus in the flesh. Philip introduced the Ethiopian to Jesus on a desert road in Gaza. The eunuch accepted Christ, was baptized in water in the desert, and went home rejoicing (Acts 8:38)! In the same manner, the jailor who imprisoned Paul and Silas accepted Christ and was instantly transformed. His sins were washed away, and he washed the wounds of the apostles (Acts 16:33–34)! The largest portion of the New Testament was written by Paul the persecutor who met Jesus and became the persecuted.

The change that Jesus facilitates in the lives of believers normally manifests in the decisions and choices they make. This is where Christian education becomes significant. Christian education must equip Christians to make decisions and choices that will glorify God. A Christian must exhibit a lifestyle that is different from that of a non-Christian. Ultimately, an individual's lifestyle is the outcome of the decisions and choices he or she makes. The Bible gives examples of good and bad decisions and choices. For example, Cain made a bad decision to worship with a wrong motive (Gen. 4). Esau decided to sell his birthright (Gen. 25:29–34), and Samson chose to confess the secret of his strength to Delilah (Judg. 16:15–17). King Saul decided to disobey God and keep the enemy alive (1 Sam. 15:20). The rich young ruler decided to walk away from the invitation given by Jesus (Matt. 19:16–22). Demas decided to forsake Paul because he chose to love the world (2 Tim. 4:10), and Governor Felix chose not to make a decision for Christ (Acts 24:24–26).

Thankfully, the Bible presents clear instructions about the healthy choices Christians must make. They are to choose unity rather than division (Ps. 133:1); forgiveness rather than bitterness (Matt. 6:12); holiness is a better choice than worldliness (1 Pet. 1:16). Love is better than hatred (1 John 4:7–8), and healing is better than brokenness (John 5:6).

Psychologists were not the first ones to say that happiness is a choice; the Bible also teaches this principle. The apostle Paul pleaded with the Philippian believers to choose happiness, saying "Rejoice in the Lord always. I will say it again: Rejoice!" (Phil. 4:4). In the Old Testament, Joshua made the most important decision: "We will serve the Lord" (Josh. 24:15).

Many churchgoers are simply cultural Christians. It is the duty of Christian educators to raise the level of biblical literacy and Christian discipleship in the churches. Seminary professors have noticed an astounding level of biblical illiteracy in incoming students, which appears to be a national problem. The remedy can only spring out of the local church, which must raise up disciples of Jesus Christ who know the Word of God so well that they are able to evaluate their culture and make truly Christian decisions on a daily basis. Sometimes the word *decision* in the Christian vocabulary is limited to the decision to accept Christ, but Christians must be trained to make healthy decisions throughout their lives. The church must equip believers to make morally right decisions; only competent, Spirit-filled Christian education can accomplish this awesome task.

Types of Faith

Charles Farah, former professor of Theology at Oral Roberts University, discussed several types of faith in believers. He did not call his model "Stages of Faith," because he felt that they were not in a hierarchy. The first type is *historical faith*. For example, a person claims to be a Baptist because his or her grandparents were Baptists, but he or she possesses no deeper reasons for his or her claim. Next is *temporary faith,* which is evident in people who become excited about a spiritual experience for a short time and then lose their enthusiasm. Instead of moving from grace to grace, these individuals go from crusade to crusade. The third type of faith is *saving faith.* When a person repents and accepts Christ as Savior, he or she experiences saving faith. The fourth category of faith is called *faith for miracles.* This type of faith is not a gift of God; rather it is something the person must work up. The fifth type, *gift faith,* is listed among the gifts of the Spirit in 1 Corinthians 12. The next type, based on the fruits of the Spirit in Galatians, is called *fruit faith.* Farah calls the final type of faith *ministry faith.* He asserts that every believer is given a measure of faith, according to Romans 12, to minister to others in whatever capacity God has called him or her to minister. Farah believes that a true disciple should function at this level of faith.

The best type of faith is not faith that simply ministers to the individual Christian; according to Farah, it is the faith that makes one reach out to others. This concept holds significant implications for the ministry of education in the church. Christians must be taught to live out their discipleship through teaching, training, and modeling. Christian education should enable believers to understand their faith to the degree that they can apply it in their daily lives, as they walk in the path of Christ through the power of the Holy Spirit.

Theological Reflection

A very old man and an infant are brought to a hospital at the same time with a severe asthma attack. Both need assistance in breathing, but the hospital only has one respiratory machine. If you were the doctor responsible to decide which patient should receive the only machine available, who would you give the machine to? The infant has his or her entire life before him or her, and the old man has lived a long time already. How would you make that decision as a Spirit-filled Christian?

A rich man who has several living children dies and leaves some artificially created embryos behind, in frozen condition, for future development. His wife wants to develop the embryos into children after the man has been dead for a while, but the living children are against the idea because they will have to share their inheritance with the children to be developed from the embryos. Should the mother be allowed to carry out her plan, or should the embryos be destroyed?

A cancer patient cannot take the pain of the disease anymore. A doctor is willing to help him or her become free from the pain through suicide. How would you respond to this doctor if you were a doctor or nurse working with him or her?

These are no longer hypothetical situations; they are real-life situations brought to us by rapidly advancing technology. The same modern science that brought us satellite communication, social media, multimedia entertainment, and many conveniences has also created these very difficult ethical dilemmas. How should we respond and make decisions regarding these situations as Spirit-led Christians?

There was a time when we could look for a proof text from scripture to find an answer. The Word of God is still the same; it still contains the answers to all human situations, but we no longer have the luxury of simply finding a random verse to apply to various complex situations. For instance, the Bible does not say, "Thou shall not watch vulgar music television" or "Thou shall not commit assisted suicide."

There are still many Christians, particularly Pentecostals and Charismatics, who insist that a proof text can be found to solve every problem. They will often take verses out of context in order to argue their points. Although there are plenty of clear directives and commands given in God's Word, many of the dilemmas facing modern believers come in subtle and complex forms. Simplistic solutions will not clearly address the issues in these situations.

The discipline of theological reflection is needed to help believers find answers for difficult questions. Theological reflection is the spiritual discipline of looking at any experience or cultural situation through the prism of God's Word, illuminated by the Holy Spirit who is working within history, tradition, and the community of faith. This is a fancy way to say that in order to know what to do in a difficult and unclear situation we must seek the teaching of the Word of God and the guidance of the Holy Spirit. We should not simply look for verses to quote, but rather, we should listen to the principles and wholesome directives of the Word of God that can assist us in making decisions that will please the Lord.

God has not left us alone; He has promised to be with us as the living Word, who has given us the written Word. He has also made us members of His body where we can depend on one another. Therefore, instead of using proof texts in isolation, we must seek the will of God in prayer, reflection, meditation, and consultation with the people of God. God will reveal His will to us through His Word, His Spirit, and His people.

Theological reflection is not for the impatient. Unless a believer receives a word of wisdom or knowledge from the Holy Spirit, it takes time to discern the will of God in difficult situations. To do this well, one must study the Word of God regularly and know what is written in the Word. Only those who know what is in the Word can look for words, metaphors, images, and directives that inform and guide in the decision-making process.

God's direction for certain issues is given directly in the Bible; however, for many modern dilemmas the answer must be discerned through theological reflection. On the occasions that immediate answers are required, the Holy Spirit can give us the gifts of the Spirit, such as the word of wisdom and the word of knowledge.

Certain historic Christian churches, which may not claim to be Charismatic, possess a long history of theological reflection. Conversely, Pentecostals and Charismatics who claim to be Spirit-filled are not generally known for their discipline of theological reflection. Lack of theological reflection is the fault of the believer, not the Holy Spirit. Believers are the ones who need to practice the disciplines of prayer, reflection, and meditation. Consistent study of the Word of God is the most important prerequisite for theological reflection. Focused study of the Bible through a well-designed Christian education program must become a vital part of all churches and ministries. Churches must prepare Spirit-filled Christians to discover the answers to the complicated questions posed to them by modern civilization. As believers learn to reflect on God's Word, through the leading of the Holy Spirit, they will discover the divine solutions to the challenging issues that are facing them daily.

Church as a Theological Seminary

The relationship between the local church and the education of future ministers has generated much discussion. Traditional seminaries and Bible colleges have been under attack for their lack of connection with the local church. Seminaries throughout the world are dealing with this issue and proposing changes to address it. I know of seminaries that are making significant changes in their curriculums and academic procedures to ensure that seminaries and churches influence one another.

Some have called for the elimination of traditional seminaries, which offer accredited theological education. I believe that accredited theological education is important, but seminaries and local churches should attempt a joint effort to provide the best training possible. I am of the opinion that the local church should provide the basic level of theological training to all believers, especially future ministers. All Christians need theological education because many are confused about what they believe. Their confusion will only increase as New Agers continue to adopt traditionally Christian terminology to mean totally different things. Only intentional and systematic study of the Bible and doctrines will equip believers to recognize false gods and doctrines. Although seminaries can be a great resource for the local church in this matter, the church must take responsibility to provide such training. Those church members who plan for full-time professional Christian ministry can seek further education in Bible colleges and seminaries.

In *The Ideal Seminary,* author and theological educator Carnegie Samuel Calian shares similar sentiments. He states:

> Theological wisdom is above all a gift to the learned and unlearned by the grace of God. Realizing once again that we are all recipients of God's grace should especially humble those of us who are theological educators ... We operate our schools, teach, write our books, and seek accreditation as if it all depends on us, the stakeholders, when in reality it all depends on the Spirit of God who imparts divine wisdom that empowers us to fulfill our destiny and equips us with a message of hope for a society in search of its soul.[9]

I share this observation to point out the importance of Christian education in the local church, not to attack academic theological education. The church cannot afford to fail in this regard because its future depends on it. Calian called theological faculty to become students again in order to improve the quality of seminary teaching. Similarly, I call pastors to become students again for the purpose of becoming better teachers. According to Calian, when faculty members become students again, the following good things will happen:

1. They will value diversity more.
2. They will no longer be lecture-bound.
3. They will provide more opportunities for students to learn experientially.
4. They will use diverse materials, such as case studies, computer networking, video films, tapes, drama, readings, and students' past experiences to create exciting teachable moments.
5. They will employ more team teaching.

I wish to see the same things in the local churches.

Chapter 7
Healing Ministry in the New Century

> Heal the sick, raise the dead, cleanse those who have leprosy,
> drive out demons. Freely you have received; freely give.
> —Matthew 10:8

Jesus commissioned His disciples to preach, teach, and heal. Healing has been part of the gospel from the very beginning and, in spite of controversies throughout the ages, it has remained a significant function and ministry of the Christian church. As excellent books on the history of healing are now available, I will not attempt to present a historical defense of the healing ministry here. My focus is the biblical, theological, and practical aspects of healing.

Healing, according to the Bible, involves wholeness. Wholeness is the opposite of brokenness, which represents the condition of fallen humanity. While the secular concept of healing can be reduced to a condition without symptoms of illness or disease, the biblical concept represents wellness, balance, and harmony. The Old Testament idea of *shalom* (peace) and the New Testament idea of *soteria* (salvation) both represent wholeness.

We were created as whole persons in the image and likeness of God, but sin brought brokenness and alienation from God into our lives. God's ultimate plan for fallen humanity is that we would be restored and reconciled to Him. To be whole is to be in sound condition, well, happy, prosperous, and peaceful. Wholeness happens through Jesus Christ, as He restores all that was lost through Adam (Rom. 5:17–21; 2 Cor. 5:17–21). Jesus came to seek and to save (Luke 19:10), to "preach good news to the poor ... to proclaim freedom for the prisoners and recovery of sight for the blind" (Luke 4:18). Humanity's healing was Jesus's mission.

The Bible clearly expresses God's intention to heal His people in both the Old and New Testaments. God's nature bears witness that healing is His good pleasure. God the healer (Ex. 15:26) loved us (John 3:16) and gave Himself for us. "Surely he took our infirmities and carried our sorrows ... and by his wounds we are healed," says Isaiah about the suffering servant (Isa. 53:4–5). Believers are advised to call the elders of the church when they are sick so that they can receive anointing with oil and prayer for their healing (James 5:13–16).

Jesus healed the sick during His earthly ministry, and He is the same yesterday, today, and forever (Heb. 13:8). However, healing of the body was not the only concern Jesus had while He lived on earth; He still desires to heal all areas of our lives—body, mind, spirit, relationships, and every other aspect. Paul emphasizes this truth in 1 Thessalonians as he says, "May your whole spirit, soul and body be kept blameless at the coming of our Lord Jesus Christ" (1 Thess. 5:23). Well-being and wholeness is God's will for humankind, and He has facilitated this through the life, death, resurrection, and ascension of Jesus Christ.

The Bible mentions several methods of healing, including calling for the elders, anointing with oil, the laying on of hands, and prayer. Jesus Himself ministered healing in many ways. He healed by pronouncing a word (John 5:8), by touching people (Matt. 8:15), and by praying, as He did at the tomb of Lazarus (John 11:41–42). There is a record that He occasionally used spittle (Mark 7:33) or instructed individuals to act certain ways by faith (John 5:8). On other occasions He healed individuals whose loved ones came to Jesus on their behalf (Matt. 8:10–13). Paul's words concerning the Lord's Supper in his first letter to the Corinthians seem to imply that the sacraments have a healing capacity (1 Cor. 11:27–32). According to scripture, God is a good God (Ps. 118:1) who is the giver of all good gifts (James 1:17). It is not accidental that healing is listed among the gifts of the Spirit in 1 Corinthians (1 Cor. 12:7–11).

The very design of the human body suggests that our welfare is important to God because we are fearfully and wonderfully made. Modern science is amazed at humankind's built-in immune system that not only prevents illnesses, but also has the power to cure diseases. It is no wonder the church has confessed the healing power of Jesus's name for two thousand years. The scriptures, the apostolic fathers, and the entire history of the church bear witness to God's power and His willingness to heal. We have no reason not to believe in healing and divine health.

The preventive health principles found in the Old Testament present persuasive evidence for the modern person that it is God's will for human beings to be healthy. For instance, the Old Testament recommends sanitation (Ex. 29:14), cleansing (Lev. 15), isolation (Num. 5:4), hygiene (Lev. 11), dietary regulations (Lev. 11), physical exercise (Gen. 3:19), and rest (Ex. 20:8–11). As the following passages illustrate, health and healing receive significant attention in the Bible. "I will take away sickness from among you" (Ex. 23:25); "A righteous man may have many troubles, but the Lord delivers him from them all" (Ps. 34:19); "Who forgives all your sins and heals all your diseases" (Ps. 103:3); "He sent forth his word and healed them; he rescued them from the grave" (Ps. 107:20). Many Old Testament figures experienced healing: Miriam was healed of leprosy (Num. 12:12–15), scores of people looked upon the serpent of brass in the wilderness and were healed of venomous snakebites (Num. 21:9), Naaman was healed of leprosy (2 Kings 5:1–15), and Job received healing from deadly sores (Job 42:10–13).

Various forms of healing occur in scripture. In the Old Testament, many barren women were healed, and several people were raised from the dead. The New Testament also documents a cloud of witnesses who received healing through the ministry of Jesus. Healing accounts in scripture did not end with Jesus's ministry; healing continued throughout the lives of the apostles. Scores of individuals in the New Testament received healing through the ministry of the apostles.

Faith and Healing

The relationship between faith and healing is often debated and considered unclear in some church traditions. As a result, people are often blamed for not receiving their healing or accused of not having enough faith. This pattern of blaming the victim is not supported by the Word of God.

Faith has been defined as seeing the invisible, believing the incredible, and accomplishing the impossible. According to the Bible, those who come to God must believe that He is, and that He rewards those who diligently seek Him (Heb. 11:6). Faith is listed among the gifts of the Spirit, as well as among the fruits of the Spirit, and Jesus related faith to healing on many occasions (Matt. 8:10, 13, 9:22, 29; Mark 5:34, 10:52). Although He rebuked individuals with little faith (Matt. 14:31; Mark 4:40; Luke 8:25), it was generally not in relation to healing. In Matthew 17, Jesus named unbelief as one factor hindering deliverance and recommended fasting and prayer.

The Bible refers to at least six modes of healing: (1) due to the patient's faith, (2) due to the faith of those who brought the patient to Jesus, (3) due to anointing and laying on of hands, (4) due to confession, (5) through casting out of spirits, and (6) through miracles. The Bible also speaks of different dimensions of faith, such as a measure of faith (Rom. 12:3) and fullness of faith (Acts 6:5, 8, 11:24). Faith comes by hearing (Rom. 10:17); faith justifies (Rom. 5:1), purifies (Acts 15:9), and sanctifies (Acts 26:18). We must live by faith (Rom. 1:17), walk by faith (2 Cor. 5:7), work by faith (2 Thess. 1:11), overcome by faith (1 John 5:4), pray by faith (James 5:15), and be healed by faith (Acts 14:9).

Although faith is a necessary element for an individual to be healed, the burden of faith is not on the patient but on the community of faith. It is wonderful when the patient believes; however, when he or she is weak or lacking in faith the community should not waste time blaming or accusing this individual. Instead, it should rise up, stand in the gap, and declare like the apostle Paul in the endangered ship: "For I (we) believe God."

The testimony of Oral Roberts is relevant here. He was healed from tuberculosis in his youth. Later, God used him as a healing evangelist. I have been a part of his ministry. Oral Roberts University grew out of the fires of healing evangelism that enveloped America and many other nations a few decades ago.

Millions of people attended the healing crusades conducted by Oral Roberts, which were held in massive tents across America and other nations. Thousands of individuals reported that they were healed from various types of illnesses at these meetings. Roberts preached the simple message that God is a good God, and that He wants to heal people. In spite of much persecution, his message resonated well with people in need across the world. The tent ministry evolved into a television ministry that was for many years the number one syndicated religious program on television in the country. I have seen his ministry receiving numerous medically documented healing testimonies annually.

Oral Roberts was foremost among the healing evangelists of the twentieth century. Others have followed him. God seems to use some of His servants to minister healing to His people to a greater extent than He uses others. However, the whole counsel of God points out that all Spirit-filled believers are capable of receiving healing and ministering healing to others.

Pastors and evangelists who minister healing must encourage people to believe God with all their hearts, because faith pleases God (Heb. 11:6). It is important that ministers understand the role of faith in healing. Jesus taught, "Everything is possible for him who believes" (Mark 9:23); "And these signs will accompany those who believe" (Mark 16:17).

Signs and Wonders

Howard Ervin's last published work was a definitive work on healing entitled *Healing: Sign of the Kingdom*. This title summarizes the testimony of Ervin and his colleagues at Oral Roberts University Seminary. A biblical scholar of great repute, Ervin concluded that signs and wonders still follow the preaching of the gospel; they confirm the good news. God does not perform miracles to entertain believers, but as a sign to the unbelievers to confirm His Word. Signs and wonders manifest the power of the kingdom of God, but Ervin discouraged believers from merely seeking signs. Believers should learn the mysteries of the kingdom of God through the teachings of Jesus so they can live as disciples engaged in kingdom business.

Portions of the foreword I composed for Ervin's book are given below, as they shed some light on the issue at hand:

> In *Healing: Sign of the Kingdom,* Professor Howard Ervin reflects biblically and theologically on the healing ministry of Jesus and the apostles ... Ervin sees healing as a vital part of Jesus' tri-fold ministry of preaching, teaching, and healing. Healing is a sign of the kingdom of God; it manifests the power of God's reign ... Signs follow the proclamation of the gospel and they confirm the message of the kingdom of God. Signs are for the unbelievers. Believers do not need signs, but they can receive healing as gifts of love from their Father ... According to Ervin, the faith that heals is the faith that saves, and the faith that saves is the faith that heals.

I believe that both Ervin's affirmation and caution are valid. We should have healing services for believers and expect that miracles will happen as signs to the unbelievers. We need to train church members to move beyond the level of seeking signs to maintaining their faith. The words of the book of Hebrews apply to us today:

> In fact, though by this time you ought to be teachers, you need someone to teach you the elementary truths of God's word all over again. You need milk, not solid food! Anyone

who lives on milk, being still an infant, is not acquainted with the teaching about righteousness. But solid food is for the mature, who by constant use have trained themselves to distinguish good from evil. (Heb. 5:12-14)

Evangelistic Versus Pastoral Healing

I believe that there are evangelistic and pastoral approaches to healing. People who do not recognize this distinction seem to attack one form or the other. The truth is that both, when conducted under the guidance of the Holy Spirit, are valid forms of healing ministry. We need to recognize that God in His wisdom gave the church apostles, prophets, evangelists, pastors, and teachers. Not all of the needs of His body can be met by individuals in one particular function of ministry; all offices are needed to equip the saints for the work of service.

God frequently uses evangelists to minister healing to His people. Evangelists often do not develop the same type of relationship with the individuals to whom they minister that a pastor must have. The ministry of evangelism is based on the needs of people and focused on evangelistic preaching. The evangelist may apply any of the biblical methods for healing because God honors His Word and heals the sick. Pastoral care, however, is a field that deals with the relational aspect of healing ministry. Pastors are shepherds called by God to care for His people, and they have a unique relationship with the people under their care. Although they may use the same biblical healing methods as the evangelists, the relational dynamic will play a role in the healing process.

According to theologians William Clebsch and Charles Jaekle, the ministry of pastoral care deals with healing, guiding, sustaining, and reconciling.[1] Thomas Oden considers it a ministry of listening, understanding, and comforting.[2] Pastors must practice what is called the incarnational presence ministry. The minister seeks to be intentionally present with the individual in need as if Christ Himself is present with him. Pastors may also occasionally have to confront people through a ministry called *carefrontation*, in which one must speak truth in love. Here one would point out, in a confidential and loving way, some of the problems or lifestyle issues that may be contributing to an individual's illness, if that person is seeking healing.

The focus of pastoral healing ministry is prayer. According to a model developed at Oral Roberts University, pastoral healing ministry includes the following steps: *Incarnational Presence, Listening, Information Gathering, Prayer,* and *Referral. Follow up* is also a part of this model.

Ted Estes, a pastor in Claremore, Oklahoma, studied the John Wimber model of healing for his Doctor of Ministry research project. He recommends a model with the following steps: *Interview, Clarification and Diagnostic Decision; Prayer Selection; Prayer;* and *Reflection*. Father Francis MacNutt, a Charismatic healing minister and former Catholic priest, offered a model called Soaking Prayer, which involves laying on of hands and having extended focused prayer for persons with serious illnesses.

Theological Presuppositions

As presented in my previous work on pastoral care, *Ministry between Miracles,* a pastoral ministry of healing is based on certain presuppositions.[3] The first assumption is that health and illness are both dynamic in nature. Health is not merely the absence of illness, but a wholeness of being. Wholeness is the aspect of human nature that defies fragmentation in body, mind, and spirit.

A second assumption is that human beings are unitary. In other words, the human body, mind, and spirit are fearfully and wonderfully interwoven at profoundly deep levels. Each aspect of human life interacts with and influences every other aspect, which means that when one part of a person is hurting, he or she hurts throughout his or her body, mind, and spirit.

This leads to a third assumption that the individual is able, knowingly or unknowingly, to affect his or her own state of wellness or illness. Personal attitudes, habits of discipline, priorities, and choices are significantly related to one's wholeness or lack of health. The faith or personal theology of an individual is a potential resource for health or a hindrance to wellness. For example, one individual's theology may burden him or her with guilt and condemnation, while another individual's theology sets him or her free from condemnation.

A Spirit-led ministry of pastoral healing is based on the following additional theological presuppositions:

- God is a good God, and He wants us to be whole. The New Testament word *soteria*, like the Old Testament word *shalom*, connotes salvation, healing, preservation, and harmony in relationships.
- God is the source of *all* healing. Whether healing results from medical intervention, faith-filled thoughts and prayer, natural biological restorative processes, or a combination of these, all healing comes from God. Growing up in a Pentecostal church that did not rely much on medical healing, I personally found this teaching initially articulated by Oral Roberts to be revelatory and freeing.
- Divine intervention in the lives of individuals in need is always a real possibility. This cannot be guaranteed for

each person in terms of time and place, but it can certainly be expected. A minister can sincerely pray for divine interventions or miracles, and it is safe to assume that God can and may intervene at any point to bring about the kind of healing that He wants in any particular situation. This is why the New Testament commands us to pray and have faith for healings.

- Healing takes various forms. Sometimes healing comes instantaneously, and at other times it comes more gradually. Sometimes healing comes as a consequence of medical intervention and sometimes as a result of prayer. Ultimately, all believers are healed at the resurrection.
- Healing is for wholeness, not for perfection. True wholeness, because it involves body, mind, and spirit, issues from a Christ-centered life of discipleship.
- Wholeness involves every aspect of one's life: physical, spiritual, emotional, relational, economic, and environmental.
- There is a reality called the fullness of time (*kairos*). Miracles occur in the fullness of time.
- Healing is enhanced by the things that nourish the spirit, such as love (1 John 4:7), hope (Ps. 42:5, 11), faith (Matt. 9:22), the will to live (John 5:6), and laughter (Phil. 4:4).
- The body of Christ is entrusted with the ministry of healing and must guard against inadvertently promoting illness.
- Pastoral counseling is extended altar ministry.
- Christian love heals. The miracle that changed the life of the Samaritan woman was that Jesus accepted her even though He knew everything she had ever done (John 4:29).

- Caring heals. True caring happens when one is willing to give up one's own agenda to consider the agenda of another, as Christ did when He gave himself for us (Phil. 2:6, 7).
- Persons engaged in the healing ministry of Jesus must consider that their own divinely formed self is a sign and wonder of God.

Pastoral healing ministry is an extension of the ministry of Jesus. In a place of pain, such as a hospital, a minister must represent the presence of Jesus. Inhabited by the life-giving Spirit of Jesus, a minister can be an incarnational presence to hurting people, a "living reminder of Jesus," as Henri Nouwen would say; he is an individual whose life reminds others of Jesus of Nazareth. Motivated by God's love and enabled by His Spirit, a caregiver becomes a channel of God's grace. As he or she ministers in the name of Christ, this grace impacts other people's lives.

A minister of the gospel has certain resources at his or her disposal. Primary among these resources is the minister's own identity as a person saved by the grace of God and filled with the Holy Spirit. William Hulme describes other powerful resources, including prayer, faith, sacraments, scripture, counseling skills, and the Christian community.[4] One can rely on personal resources and pastoral authority to establish healing relationships. The Holy Spirit will work in and through these relationships to bring healing and wholeness to persons.

Healing Ministry in the Local Church

The local church of the twenty-first century should be a healing place. Although our world is more secularized and generally hostile to religion in many ways, discussion of spiritual matters is more acceptable today. Research on the impact of prayer and meditation on cardiac patients, nuns, and Buddhist monks has opened even the secular mind to the power of prayer, albeit any type of prayer. The church should take advantage of this openness to teach people about faith in Jesus Christ and prayer in the name of Jesus. Many people coming to the churches are wounded and fragmented; therefore, the church must offer them more than a message on positive thinking. We have something powerful to offer people for the healing of body, mind, spirit, finances, and relationships. Much of what the church offers is preventive. Preventive teaching on moral commandments and instructions concerning the care and discipline of the body are important contributions for maintaining physical healing. Opportunities for forgiveness in relationships, the development of the fruits of the Spirit, and the possibility of renewing one's mind are very important preventive measures for maintaining healing of the mind. The good news of eternal life, opportunities to worship, the gifts of the Spirit, the resources of the community of faith, and the privilege of prayer are contributions the church can make for spiritual well-being.

The church possesses many resources for its curative work, including the utilization of the elders of the church to anoint the sick and pray for them, the sacraments as instruments of healing, professional as well as pastoral counseling, instruction in whole person lifestyle, prayer partners and altar counselors, healing services, hospital ministry, and even ongoing healing schools. The church can sponsor healing crusades inside and outside of its walls and can invite evangelists to minister to the people. Pastors and evangelists working together can enhance the ministry of healing in the local church. Healing crusades provide evangelistic opportunities as people hear the gospel and see the power of the Spirit manifesting in signs, wonders, and miracles. The local church must support missionary evangelists and healing ministers in order to expand the ministry of the church to the community and the world.

Unfortunately, there are still churches that do not teach about the healing ministry of Jesus. There are others that talk about it but never practice it. The new century calls for churches that will teach and practice healing ministry. Our world desperately needs healing, and many in the churches are also hurting badly. The church should not wait for medical doctors to do all the healing work; ministers and physicians must complement one another's work. I am very grateful to Oral Roberts for his pioneering work in merging medicine and prayer at the former City of Faith Medical and Research Center in Tulsa, Oklahoma. Doctors, nurses, and ministers worked hand-in-hand at the City of Faith to bring healing to patients who had come from all over the world. Roberts pioneered the concept of healing teams that included doctors, nurses, ministers, and other professionals. As a Pentecostal/Charismatic, he was open to the contributions of the medical field, and at the same time he believed in the power of the Holy Spirit to bring healing and wholeness to people. As a chaplain and prayer partner at the hospital in the 1980s, I witnessed the power of the Holy Spirit working though these healing teams.

Although the City of Faith closed, physicians who were trained there still spread the message of whole person healing throughout the world. Many medical schools and hospitals are now practicing what was taught at the City of Faith concerning whole person healing; these ideas were considered novel when the City of Faith implemented them. At a time when Pentecostals and Charismatics were hostile toward medicine, Oral Roberts had the courage to declare that all healing is from God. His bold stand freed a great number of Pentecostals to receive healing regardless of the avenue through which it came. May this legacy of whole person healing continue through the graduates of Oral Roberts University and the readers of these pages.

Chapter 8
Empowered Servant Leadership

> And whoever wants to be first must be slave of all.
> —Mark 10:44

Much misunderstanding exists in the body of Christ concerning ministerial leadership. Often perceptions of ministry and leadership are based on people's personal experiences with ministers and, unfortunately, not all such experiences are positive, causing many to hold seriously distorted views of Christian leadership. I am reminded of one leader who commented to me about his relationship with his associates, "I don't have headaches, Tom; I give headaches!" Our definitions of ministry and leadership should come from the Word of God, not from wounded persons.

Ministry leadership does not depend on the natural talents of ministerial candidates because God can use both our strengths and our weaknesses in His service. When God called Moses, he did not present his qualifications to God; instead, he acknowledged that he could not speak eloquently. Jeremiah presented his inability to speak as an excuse; when God called Saul to be the first king of Israel, he acknowledged his humble family of origin. None of these individuals claimed their competence or worthiness, yet today we seem to think of people with talent as the best candidates for ministry and leadership. God-given talents have their place in ministry, but talents do not make the real difference; God's call and an individual's obedience to that call are the crucial factors in effective ministry leadership.

The apostle Paul makes it very clear that ministry is service. He uses the term *servant* or *slave* to describe himself, stating that he is a servant of the Lord (Rom. 1:1), a servant of the church (2 Cor. 11:8), and a servant of the gospel (Phil. 2:22). Ministry is servant leadership that involves offering one's service to God and humankind. Spirit-filled ministry is servant leadership empowered by the Holy Spirit.

Many have written about the topic of Christian leadership. According to Bruce Goettsche, Christian leaders have the following characteristics: they love people, they have a servant attitude, they are honest, they think big, they fight for the ones in need, they build people up, and they give the best they have.[1] All Christian leaders can adopt these good qualities; a greater challenge, however, is to be a Spirit-filled servant leader.

Next Stage of Leadership

Even the secular world is pointing out the need for behavioral changes among leaders. For example, changes are taking place in the area of nonprofit leadership. According to Warren Bennis and Burt Nanus, nonprofit leadership is entering a new stage where, for instance, leadership is distributed at all levels of the institution, effectiveness is more important than efficiency, anticipating change is better than adapting to change, empowering is better than directing, and coaching is better than bossing.[2]

In his book *The Young Evangelicals,* Robert Webber of Northern Baptist Theological Seminary in Lombard, Illinois, talks about a new paradigm of church and leadership. According to Webber, the church should be a community that prefers relationship to anonymity.[3] This implies that Christian worship must change from a mere program to actual interaction, and spirituality must shift from obedience to external things to living by internal convictions. Webber says that pastors must move from exercising personal power to offering servanthood in the area of leadership, and ministerial leaders must give priority to relationship building and transformation of persons.

Biblical Language of Leadership

The language of leadership in modern church circles seems to be dominated by secular concepts and models. For instance, some ministers follow an executive model in which complexity is rewarded. According to Edward B. Bratcher in *Walk on Water Syndrome,* others follow a million dollar round table model that rewards salesmanship.[4] A third model is represented by the president of a corporation who is rewarded for keeping the stockholders happy, and the "crowded calendar" model emphasizes and rewards activity. These models appear practical but not necessarily biblical. Gordon Fee in *Gospel and Spirit* encourages ministers to have a different perspective on leadership by considering the biblical language of leadership.[5] He challenges ministers to review the true meaning of the following terms: church (*ecclesia*), people (*laos*), covenant (*diatheke*), saints (*hoi hagioi*), and chosen (*eklektos*). Fee challenges Christian leaders to consider the concepts of family (2 Cor. 6:18), household (1 Tim. 3:5, 15), body (1 Cor. 10:17), temple (1 Cor. 3:16), and commonwealth (Phil. 3:20, 21). Any definition of leadership derived from these biblical terms and concepts will have the distinctiveness of Christian servant leadership.

Secrets of Success

In his biography *Expect a Miracle*, Oral Roberts shares ten secrets of his success in ministry. One can see in these statements certain theological concepts that informed his ministry leadership.

1. He learned that the message he carried was greater than his personal identity as the messenger.
2. He ensured that he was anointed each time he ministered.
3. He made it a practice to reinforce his preaching by his own personal testimony.
4. He insisted on remaining constant in his integrity and purpose.
5. He chose to work with believers who authentically believed God.
6. Through experience, he learned to identify the key issues involved in a situation. In other words, he did not major in minors.
7. He learned how to use a point of contact, which is an act that allows an individual to release his faith to accomplish God's purposes. For example, a woman who had been sick for many years reached out and touched Jesus's garment as a point of contact and was instantly healed (Mark 5:28).
8. He believed that it is possible to change methods but not principles.
9. He learned that faith is present whenever one begins to seek it.
10. He practiced sowing and reaping as a lifestyle.[6]

According to Edward B. Bratcher, ministers need certain guidelines by which to measure their success in ministry. Because of the multitude of issues they experience in ministry, it is hard to see success even when there is significant progress. The following guidelines can be used to measure success:

1. Define the meaning of one's ministry.
2. Define success for oneself.
3. Break down major goals into measurable goals.
4. Avoid comparing one's ministry with the ministry of another.
5. Consider the goals of ministry, the gifts of ministry, and the context of ministry.
6. Include spiritual goals.
7. Clarify the goals of the institution as opposed to one's own goals.
8. Do actual study of progress or lack thereof.
9. Have services of celebration for smaller achievements.
10. Keep a daily journal to document ongoing ministry.[7]

Ministers will benefit from remembering the words of the apostle Paul, "Therefore, my beloved brethren, be steadfast, immovable, always abounding in the work of the Lord, knowing that your labor is not in vain in the Lord" (1 Cor. 15:58 NKJV).

Management and Conflict Resolution

John Kotter, a professor at Harvard Business School, differentiated management from leadership in his book *Leading Change*. According to Kotter, management has to do with planning and budgeting, while leadership has to do with establishing direction for an organization.[8] Managers organize and staff an organization, while leaders communicate direction to people. In Kotter's view, controlling and problem solving are management duties; leaders are called to motivate and inspire followers.

Although ministry is God's work, it often causes conflicts among people, and ministers find themselves in the middle of such conflicts. Most ministers are not comfortable handling conflicts, so they tend to avoid or deny them. Some try to cope by belittling the problem, while others try to resolve the issue by arguing in a destructive fashion. The goal of a leader should be to approach problems in a constructive way through one of the many models of conflict resolution. The following outlines one such model developed by Kenneth O. Gangel.

1. Classify and define the problem.
2. Develop criteria for a successful solution.
3. Generate alternatives.
4. Compare alternatives to criteria.
5. Choose an alternative.
6. Implement the decision.
7. Monitor the decision and get feedback.[9]

This conflict resolution model is very similar to the problem solving model presented by John Lawyer in his book *Communication Skills for Ministry*.

1. Identify a problem in terms of desired outcome.
2. Identify all possible options and clarify them.
3. Evaluate every option.
4. Decide on an acceptable option.
5. Develop an implementation plan that should answer the questions: What? Who? Resources? Time?
6. Develop an evaluation strategy.
7. Review the experience.[10]

Limits of Ministry Leadership

Ministers must deal with many personal limitations in the face of unlimited demands placed on them in ministry leadership. If a minister can develop the skill of time management, he or she will be able to balance the limited amount of time available to do all that is required. This involves the art of self-limitation. Ministers must face limited energy, because ministry is never really finished. When a minister attempts to finish the work in order to gain a sense of completion, he or she is likely to experience a sense of failure. It is better to conserve one's energy by dealing with priorities based on one's values. Ministers also contend with the limitations of knowledge. No leader possesses knowledge of everything that needs to be known; therefore, he or she must be a lifelong learner, continuously improving his or her knowledge base. Ministers can attempt to utilize other persons as resources in the area of knowledge. For example, seminaries and Bible colleges offer educational experiences for ministers, but they can also be sources of expert knowledge for local ministries. Ministry leadership also confronts individuals with limitations in the area of achievement; a minister cannot base his or her sense of well-being on accomplishments. Ministers can periodically celebrate smaller achievements to remind themselves that they are moving toward bigger goals.

Effective Leadership

J. Robert Clinton lists seven leadership lessons he has observed emerging in his classes:

1. Effective leaders maintain a learning posture throughout life.
2. Effective leaders value spiritual authority as a primary power base.

3. Effective leaders recognize leadership selection and development as a priority function.
4. Effective leaders view relational empowerment as both a means and a goal of ministry.
5. Effective leaders who are productive over a lifetime have a dynamic ministry philosophy.
6. Effective leaders evidence a growing awareness of their sense of destiny.
7. Effective leaders increasingly perceive their ministry in terms of a lifetime perspective instead of a hit and run.[11]

Henri Nouwen has much to say about ministry leadership. He believes that the minister, as a servant leader, is called to be a wounded healer whose wounds become a source of healing for others.[12] Nouwen is careful to delineate the difference between wounded healers and bleeding healers. A bleeding healer is one who is still hurting from his or her own injuries and disappointments, whereas a wounded healer is in the process of advancing toward wholeness. A wounded healer carries scars, but they are not bleeding; as a result, the wounded healer is able to focus on others and minister to them. Nouwen's perspective is a sobering reminder, even to those who move in the power of the Holy Spirit, to seek personal wholeness.

According to Nouwen, a minister must be a person of prayer. No ministry can exist without prayer and the Word, because a minister must test all things by the Word of God. The Word of God is his or her standard for faith and conduct as he or she listens to the voice of the Spirit within him- or herself. The Word of God is the currency of transaction for a minister.

For Nouwen, ministry is also hospitality. A minister makes room for strangers on the couch in his or her heart, and as a good host he or she must be comfortable with him- or herself before his or her guests can feel at home. Nouwen calls the minister a living reminder of Jesus. Just as the bread and the cup of communion remind one of the life, death, and resurrection of Jesus, a minister's life, according to Nouwen, should remind people of Jesus of Nazareth. Nouwen believes that God's work is not limited to an individual's strengths; He also redeems human weaknesses and uses them for His glory. Nouwen's work does not highlight the power dimension ministry; however, the leadership model he presents can be incorporated into a Spirit-empowered model of servant leadership.

A Spirit-Led Model

The Bible frequently speaks about leaders and leadership. God the Father is a leader of His people. God the Son is a leader who invites people to follow Him. God the Holy Spirit is also a leader because the scripture admonishes Christians to "be led by the Spirit."

The Bible contains a long list of godly leaders. Abraham led his family out of a pagan land, and Joseph led the government of Egypt during a period of crisis. Moses led the people of God out of Egypt, Miriam led them in worship, and Joshua led Israel into the Promised Land. Deborah, as a judge and prophetess, was a leader of the people of God. David led as a man after God's own heart, and Elijah provided prophetic leadership during a historic period. Elisha followed in Elijah's footsteps and became a leader of prominence. Daniel was a leader with great wisdom in Babylon.

In the New Testament, Peter was a leading personality among the disciples, and Paul provided apostolic leadership to the early Church. He was an exemplary leader, who said, "Follow me as I follow Christ." Priscilla provides an example of women's leadership in the early church, and Timothy represents a young pastor/leader.

Servant leadership was prominent throughout the history of the church, beginning with the apostles and church fathers. Additionally, Saint Augustine, Martin Luther, John Calvin, John Wesley, Jonathan Edwards, Charles Finney, Charles Parham, William Seymour, Kathryn Kuhlman, and Martin Luther King, Jr. are only a few who have left their mark as leaders of the church; the list is long.

Ministerial servant leadership is different from all other forms of leadership. Jesus told His disciples that they should not "lord it over" their followers as the heathen do; leadership in ministry follows the paradigm of the kingdom of God. In God's kingdom, the leader does not give pain, he absorbs it. The shepherd does not wound the sheep; instead, he risks his life for the sheep. Leadership in God's kingdom is defined by the following values: The first shall be the last and the last shall be the first; giving is receiving, and dying is the way to live.

I have seen some exemplary leaders within the Spirit-empowered movement. Unfortunately, I have also watched some who rivaled heathens in their leadership style. Power or perceived power was a snare to these leaders, but in several cases, it turned out that they only had an illusion of power. I saw the Lord dealing with them eventually for the way they treated God's people. Some remained a mystery to me as they continued to cause pain without any apparent consequences. The worst leaders are insecure people who surround themselves with yes men and exercise great control over others. These leaders rule by manipulation and intimidation and thrive in a climate of fear and toxic faith. They use people to build things instead of building up people who would build things for them. I have noticed that leaders who use up people to build things eventually lose both people and things.

Spirit-filled servant leadership has some unique requirements. Spirit-filled leadership is service with power; Spirit-empowered leaders serve others in the name of Christ in the power of the Holy Spirit. Such leadership requires: (1) an intimate encounter with God, (2) the anointing of the Holy Spirit, and (3) a willingness to take action by faith.

Encounter with God

All godly leaders in scripture experienced an intimate encounter with the living God. God met with Abraham personally (Gen. 17:1–6), and Moses encountered Him on a mountainside in the burning bush (Ex. 3:1–7). Joshua had an experience with God after Moses died (Josh. 1:1–5), and Samuel encountered God as a young man in the temple (1 Sam. 3:4–11). Elijah encountered the Word of God as he was commanded to go and hide himself by the brook Cherith (1 Kings 17:2–3). Isaiah encountered God in the year King Uzziah died (Isa. 6:1–9), and Ezekiel encountered Him in the valley of dry bones (Ezek. 37:3).

An encounter with God is a life-transforming experience. Isaiah's experience demonstrates the framework of an encounter with God. First, Isaiah encounters the glory of God as He is seated high and lifted up in the temple. Immediately afterward, Isaiah unexpectedly recognizes impurity in himself. The unpleasantness of this experience causes him to cry out, "Woe is me. I am a man of unclean lips!" (Isa. 6:5). Isaiah recognizes that his position as a prophet involves the use of his tongue, which is found to be unclean, but God does not leave him in this condition of despair. God sends an angel with a red hot coal to touch Isaiah's lips, and he is cleansed. After the cleansing process, he has an encounter with the call of God, "Who will go for us? Whom shall we send?" Isaiah responds, "Here am I, send me" (Isa. 6:8).

Often leaders miss the second step of an encounter with God, which involves the acknowledgement of one's own inadequacies. Many overlook the mystery that God can use their weaknesses as well as their strengths. In fact, He can turn the weaknesses into strengths.

The lives of biblical leaders demonstrate that an encounter with God can truly transform a life. For instance, Abraham's life was changed in order to be a blessing to the nations, and Moses was transformed into the man who was to lead God's people out of bondage. Joshua was changed as God raised him up to lead them into the Promised Land. Samuel, Isaiah, Elijah, Ezekiel, and many others were also transformed through their encounters with the Lord.

An encounter with God can change one's identity. A person's name is a significant part of his or her identity. When an individual's name is changed, his or her identity is also changed. Jacob became Israel, Saul became Paul, and Simon became Peter.

An encounter with God also changes a person's agenda. The individual's personal goals are no longer important; he or she adopts God's goals. After the burning bush experience, Moses did not try to deliver the people his own way; he adopted God's way. The theme of a servant leader becomes, "Not my will, but thine."

Anointing of the Holy Spirit

Spirit-filled leadership requires the anointing of the Holy Spirit. Anointing here refers to the presence and power of God resting upon the leader. Personal qualities and abilities are not the most important aspects of a servant leader's work; the empowerment of the Holy Spirit makes the difference in one's service to others.

The Bible clearly illustrates this point. When King Saul disobeyed God, Samuel went to Bethlehem to anoint David as the next leader of the Israelites. Samuel invited Jesse and his sons to a place of worship (1 Sam. 16:3). Jesse's first son, Eliab, appeared to be an outstanding candidate, but the Lord said to Samuel, "Do not consider his appearance or his height ... The Lord does not look at the things man looks at. Man looks at the outward appearance, but the Lord looks at the heart" (1 Sam. 16:7). Samuel was surprised as God rejected each of Jesse's seven sons and asked, "Are these all the sons you have?" (1 Sam 16:11). When Jesse mentioned his youngest son, David, Samuel told him to send for David. When David approached, Samuel heard the Lord say, "Rise and anoint him; he is the one" (1 Sam. 16:12b). Then "Samuel took the horn of oil and anointed him in the presence of his brothers, and from that day on the Spirit of the Lord came upon David in power" (1 Sam. 16:13). David was selected by God and anointed by Samuel; the anointing brought the power of God into David's life.

Spirit-filled ministry is a power-filled ministry. The power does not stem from personal charisma, but from the power of the Holy Spirit. The *charismata*, or gifts of the Holy Spirit, are more important than personality or personal charisma. The anointing of the Holy Spirit gives the unction and empowerment for service.

The New Testament ministers were anointed by the Holy Spirit. According to the gospel of John, Jesus breathed on His disciples. The apostles were among the 120 who received the Holy Spirit in the upper room on the day of Pentecost. Paul, a latecomer, also received the baptism of the Holy Spirit prior to his apostolic ministry. Servant leadership is not powerless ministry; it is ministry in the power of the Holy Spirit. Such a ministry is available for every individual whom God chooses, regardless of his or her personal resources or charisma.

Walk by Faith

It is one thing to receive the anointing of the Holy Spirit, but it is another matter to act on it. Christian ministry is a walk of faith. This faith walk is the door that allows the Holy Spirit to manifest Himself through the life and ministry of God's servants, and it is the anointing of the Holy Spirit that leads a minister to take action by faith. The relationship between Elijah and Elisha demonstrates this concept. After Elijah trained Elisha to become a prophet, the time came for Elijah to be taken from Elisha. Elijah asked Elisha what he might do for him. Just as Solomon asked for wisdom, Elisha replied that he wanted a double portion of the Spirit that was upon Elijah. Although he could have asked for anything, Elisha asked for a double portion of the Spirit. Elijah responded that if Elisha saw him depart, he would receive his wish. Elisha followed Elijah from Gilgal to Bethel, from Bethel to Jericho, and from Jericho to the Jordan River. As Elisha watched, Elijah struck the Jordan with his mantle, and the river opened up for them to cross over to the other side. Soon after, as the senior prophet was taken up to heaven in a whirlwind, his mantle fell to the ground. The mantle was a symbol of the anointing that was upon Elijah. Elisha picked up the mantle and held it in his hand as he stood by the river. As he struck the river with the mantle, he asked, "Where is the God of Elijah?" Elisha had watched Elijah take many steps of faith; now the anointing that had rested upon Elijah had fallen upon him. It was time for him to act by faith.

Elisha knew Elijah's God, and he knew God's character. He recognized that Elijah's God was a God who spoke, and he understood that Elijah's God would be able to provide for all his needs. Elisha possessed the knowledge that Elijah's God could send rain or fire as needed and divide the river, but mere knowledge was not enough. He had to act on that knowledge under the anointing he had just received. As an act of pure faith, Elisha struck the water just as Elijah had, and it divided to the right and to the left! Just as faith without works is dead, Spirit-filled servant leadership without faith-based actions is ineffective.

The anointing of the Holy Spirit enables the Christian minister to claim the authority that belongs to him or her through the power of the Holy Spirit. When a minister walks by faith, he or she demonstrates his or her trust in the words of Jesus who said, "All authority in heaven and on earth has been given to me. Therefore go …" Elisha's life of obedience demonstrates the importance of taking leadership actions by faith. The river would not have opened if he had just stood and waited. Striking the river was the first step of a great and powerful ministry.

The book of Kings recounts the miracles Elisha performed. For example, when poisonous water was killing the land, Elisha cleansed it by adding salt. This miracle followed his first step of faith at the Jordan. Similarly, Elisha instructed Naaman, the seriously ill commander of the Syrian army, to immerse himself in the river seven times and Naaman was healed. This healing would not have occurred if Elisha had merely stood by the river holding the mantle in his hand. In the same manner, the widow whose sons were in danger of being enslaved received ministry and help from Elisha. If Elisha had not taken the first step of faith in his ministry, the desperate needs of many would not have been met.

The key to success in power-filled servant leadership requires a true encounter with the living God, the anointing of the Holy Spirit, and the willingness to step out in faith. A missionary directing a Bible college in India shared the following testimony. A recently converted young man enrolled as a student at the local Bible school. He was newly born-again, Spirit-filled, and inexperienced in ministry. As he was going by an open market one day, he saw a Hindu priest unsuccessfully attempting to cast the devil out of a young girl. As the young man passed by, he perceived God's voice in his heart saying, "You go and set that girl free." He tried to ignore the voice and kept walking, but the inner voice repeated that he had to go back. The priest gave him permission to pray for the young girl. The inexperienced Bible student laid his hand on the young girl and rebuked the evil spirit in the name of Jesus; she was instantly healed. The big commotion that followed caused him to leave the scene.

This happened during a time of great tension between Hindus and Christians in the community. As a result, the young Bible school student realized that he might be the target of retaliation by Hindu extremists. The next morning he awoke to the rumbling sound of a crowd around his little house. With fear and trembling he went to the door to see what was happening, certain that the Hindus had come to attack him. As he opened the door, he was surprised to hear the people say, "We heard that a man by the name of Jesus lives in this house, and we heard that he healed a young girl in the marketplace yesterday. We want him to come and heal these sick people too." It was not the Bible student's knowledge or expertise that broke through in that marketplace; it was his willingness to step out in faith as the Holy Spirit prompted him. He had an encounter with God and was filled with the Holy Spirit, and he acted by faith.

The twenty-first century church is seeking empowered servant leaders who will lead her to greater heights. The church needs a new generation of leaders who have encountered God, have been empowered by the Holy Spirit, and are willing to act by faith. Only with such leaders could she overcome the obstacles in her way as she journeys to the city whose builder and maker is God.

Chapter 9

Becoming a Spirit-Empowered Minister

"Come, follow me," Jesus said, "and I will
send you out to fish for people."
—Matthew 4:19

We have taken a comprehensive look at Spirit-empowered ministry in this volume. Beginning with a definition of the Christian ministry from biblical, theological, practical, and historical perspectives, this book has given considerable attention to a Spirit-empowered perspective on ministry and particularly to the four major tasks of ministry—preaching, teaching, healing, and leading. Having seen that ministry must be biblically sound, theologically balanced, professionally competent, and spiritually empowered, some readers may wonder how one may become a practitioner of such a ministry? How does a person become a Spirit-empowered minister?

These are important questions, especially for those who are sensing a call or are in preparation for ministry in a Bible college or seminary. Let me respond to these questions briefly in this final chapter.

A Call to Ministry

Any discussion about becoming a minister should begin with the idea of a call. Parents, teachers, or pastors do not call people to ministry, although all of them can influence one in positive ways in this regard. In fact, no one should venture out to enter ministry just because his or her mother or father told him or her to do so, even when the parent happens to be a minister. Bible colleges and seminaries cannot call people to ministry either; they can only train people for Christian service. It is God who calls. The first step to becoming a Spirit-empowered minister is to discern a call. God's call is not always dramatic or necessarily at a specific time and place. In some cases it may be similar to the dramatic call of Moses, Isaiah, or Paul, but in most cases it is much less sensational. In many cases it may be an unremarkable process involving very ordinary people and some divine appointments. Many people find themselves on their way to prepare for some other profession or being involved in some other business when they discern God's call.

I was studying physics with the hope of becoming a scientist when I sensed God's call. My father was trying to establish a modest business when he felt called. Having watched different people respond differently to God's call, my suggestion is to yield to the call of God as early as possible. I know individuals who disobeyed or postponed what they sensed as God's call due to family, fear, or ambitions and then were miserable later in life. I have also watched some who eventually returned to their original calling, but made themselves and others miserable by trying to overcompensate for the lost time. It is better to be like young Samuel and say, "Speak, Lord, for your servant is listening."

Remember that God's call normally follows a process, as Richard Niebuhr suggested. Pay attention to this process and don't be afraid to check with people in your life who may be able to validate your perceptions. You don't need to bargain with God as if He is calling you to some kind of misery. Discover God's will as you would in any situation and simply make yourself available to Him. Don't be drawn by perceived status or other attractions of ministry. There is nothing wrong with having a desire to be a minister because, according to Saint Paul, a person desiring to be a minister is seeking a good thing (1 Tim. 3:1); make sure that you are motivated by a desire to *serve* God and His people.

It is very unusual for someone to know God's ultimate plans for his or her life at the beginning of this process. In most cases, one has to step out in faith at some point based on the light one has received because discovering God's ultimate purpose can be a lifelong process. Recall that the apostle Paul first said that God called him on his way to Damascus (Acts 26:16). Later he stated that God called him while he was in his mother's womb (Gal. 1:15). Further down the road in his journey of faith, Paul said God's call took place before the world began (2 Tim. 1:9)! We can only conclude that the longer we serve God, the deeper we understand His plans and purposes for us. Don't be afraid to step out in faith based on what you already know. I can guarantee that this will be an exciting journey of discovery. I have never regretted not becoming a scientist. It is hard to prove, but even my study of physics and mathematics has actually helped me in fulfilling God's assignment to serve as a seminary dean.

As I speak about the call of God as a prerequisite for Spirit-empowered ministry, I am presuming that the candidate is a truly born-again person who has experienced the life transforming impact of the new birth. I am trusting that an encounter with Jesus Christ has had a profound impact on the individual and that the person is fully committed to share the gospel of the kingdom of

God with others. I take it for granted that the person is an active participant in a community of faith that offers fellowship, worship, sacraments, and nurture. I am also assuming that the person is filled with the Holy Spirit, able to pray in the Spirit and with understanding. Whether one calls it speaking in tongues or prayer language, a person desiring to be a Spirit-empowered minister must be able to pray in the Spirit and engage in such a prayer on a regular basis. Please notice that I have not recommended affiliation with a particular denomination or faith group. Although ordination is vitally important, I believe one's ecclesiastical affiliation is secondary to the things I have mentioned here.

Next is the matter of preparation for ministry. Here is the rule of thumb: Your preparation must match your calling. Once you discern your calling, you should seek counsel regarding the training required to fulfil that call adequately. Some may need only an institute level training to fulfil their calling. Others may require graduation from Bible college or seminary. Some others, like those called to seminary teaching, need doctoral level training. I do not look down on any level of ministerial training. I believe all levels of training from certificate and diploma to doctorates are needed. Your training should prepare you for your calling.

This means some of my readers will have to stay in school longer and others need to quit expensive higher education in theology. I compare the longer stay in school to the time a plane spends on the runway. Normally, larger planes needing to stay in the air longer spend more time on the runway as they take off. Smaller planes can take off faster from shorter runways, but they don't stay as long in the air or fly as high as the bigger ones. This is why discovering one's calling is such a vital step. I have seen some people staying too long in school, others leaving too soon, and yet another group refusing to enter a training process. Peter and Paul did not have the same academic preparation or capacity, but both were effective in their ministries. What is God calling you to do? Prepare for it.

Keep in mind that you don't have to be fully prepared for lifelong service at the beginning of your ministry as there are differing assignments within the same general calling. You will have opportunities to prepare more fully for special assignments as you go forward. For instance, you may begin your work as a pastor and then sense a leading to a specialized ministry such as chaplaincy or seminary teaching. I did not begin ministry expecting to be a chaplain, seminary professor, or dean. I felt a call to be a pastor, and eventually within that call, I found the other assignments. As a dean, I saw myself as a pastor to the faculty and staff, and the students at large, although my daily duties included seminary leadership and higher education administration. I became a lifelong learner and received the education and training I needed as various doors opened. God used several people to speak into my life during crucial moments in my journey. They encouraged me, mentored me, and stood by me when I needed them. They also provided me a sense of accountability. Make sure you keep some Barnabases in your life.

So far I have addressed novices; now let me turn to seasoned ministers who desire a more effective Spirit-filled ministry. It has been pointed out that a significant number of ministers are leaving the ministry due to burnout. Anyone knowing the demands of twenty-first century ministry will be sympathetic to their plight. The fact is that there is another group that may not be leaving the ministry, but remain in ministry stagnant and ineffective. These are persons who in most cases entered the vocation with much energy and enthusiasm, but ran into difficult persons, situations, or life issues. It is a great mistake to claim that one fully understands their challenges. I simply wish to mention some observations I have made of ministers who have survived such trials.

Ministers who continue their spiritual growth seem to overcome challenges better and remain effective. Here are some things that are indicative of spiritual growth in ministers. First, they have a definite sense of self. They have good personal boundaries; they know where they end and others begin. Secondly, they have a definite sense of calling and an understanding of their own strengths and weaknesses in relation to that calling. This enables them to say no when appropriate. Thirdly, they have biblically sound convictions based on a faith they own. In other words, they have a well-informed personal theology that they are able to articulate. Parroting or defending someone else's theology is extremely stressful. Fourthly, these ministers are able to handle paradoxes in their lives and ministries. They don't feel a need to explain the unexplainable and are able to say the words, "I don't know." They also don't have a need to straighten out everyone else's life or theology.

Next, ministers who overcome challenges and distress in ministry seem to be able to reinterpret or reframe their own life stories in a healthy way. They are able to reflect on their own lives and ministry experiences and allow different ways of looking at themselves as persons and ministers. Finally, there is a level of integration of life and faith in these ministers. They seek a level of congruence between their faith and lives, that is, between what they preach and what they practice.

In addition to learning about preventing or treating burnout, ministers may wish to pay attention to the healthy qualities I have listed above. However, none of these ideas matches the need to be fully open to the strength and guidance of the Holy Spirit. The bread and water Elijah received in the wilderness at a very low point in his life should remind all of us to remain open to receive the nourishment of the Word and the Spirit during the turbulent days of our lives. Perhaps, we may also be able to run for forty days and nights after that.

Ministry was never meant to be accomplished by our own strength and power. The story of David Huxley illustrates this point. Huxley beat his own record of the unusual sport of pulling airplanes at an airport in Sydney, Australia. Tying himself to the front wheel strut of a Boeing 747 jumbo jet weighing 187 tons using a fifteen-yard-long steel cable, Huxley pulled the plane one hundred yards in just one minute and twenty-one seconds! You can imagine his exhaustion and physical condition at the end of the feat. Great accomplishment, indeed, but planes are not designed to be pulled! Flying them should not physically exhaust the pilot in seconds. An experienced pilot can get the four engines of the 747 to fly at the highest levels to reach the most distant lands. Ministry is not supposed to be pulled by our own strength alone. Any attempt to do so will exhaust us. It is better to depend on the power of the Holy Spirit. If only we could learn to fly under the wings of the Holy Spirit!

A Call to Empowerment

I grew up in Pentecostal parsonages in India and lived almost all of my adult life in America. Having lived in two countries, I have had occasions to observe ministry as a participant observer in two different cultural and economic contexts. Additionally, my travels have given me many opportunities to observe Christian ministry in other nations. I can sincerely say that ministry is difficult in all contexts. The difficulties are not all the same, but challenges are universal. In all contexts and at all times, ministers who actively open their lives to the power and leading of the Holy Spirit seem to do better. Natural talents and proper training certainly make a significant difference in the quality of ministry, but what makes ministry stand out is the ministers' active dependence on the Holy Spirit.

No wonder Jesus asked His disciples to stay in Jerusalem until they were empowered. He knew the task was going to be difficult. He also knew that the disciples in their own strength were no match for the challenge. These two variables remain the same today. Ministry is meant to be empowered and guided by the Holy Spirit until the end.

I value higher education for ministry. I have spent most of my professional life investing in people who were preparing for ministry. However, training alone does not produce effective ministers. Skills can be learned. Professionalism can be developed. Effectiveness in ministry additionally requires both character and empowerment. Character deals with the fruits of the Spirit, and empowerment has to do with the gifts of the Holy Spirit. It is the Holy Spirit who makes ministry truly effective.

Ministry is a spiritual enterprise. A minister in his or her work is dealing with the issues of life and death, time and eternity, the finite and the infinite. This is the realm of the Spirit. Ministry practices disconnected from the active engagement of the Holy Spirit limit it to an ordinary helping profession. Ministry deals with revelation and mystery. Ministry deals with the natural and the supernatural. Ministry deals with the prophetic. Ministers are called to participate in the work of God in the world. This cannot be done without active dependence on the Holy Spirit.

The truth is that no one can be argued into the kingdom of God. No one can be scared into the kingdom of God. There is no foolproof apologetics. The empty tomb does not convince everyone. No amount of scientific argument can produce a convert. It is the Spirit who woos individuals to the kingdom of God. It is the Spirit who witnesses before the first missionary arrives. It is the Spirit who converts and sanctifies. The leap of faith is not just a logical conclusion. It is a step of faith, a Spirit-led activity. Ministry is utterly dependent on the Holy Spirit.

True ministry is always Pentecostal, and Pentecost deals with the presence of God. Active ministry requires the presence and power of the Holy Spirit, so I exhort you to depend on the empowerment of the Holy Spirit.

Study all you can to become a competent minister. Develop all the skills required as a pastor, priest, or evangelist, but depend on the Holy Spirit. Open your life to the life of the Spirit. Consider yourself a funnel through which God's Spirit can flow. Let ministry become an outflow of the work of the Spirit in your life. Let it flow to others in the form of competent ministry.

You cannot create revivals. You cannot manufacture signs and wonders. But you can depend on the Holy Spirit for signs, wonders, healings, and miracles. You can rejoice when they happen, but you don't take any credit for them. You don't blame yourself when they don't happen, but minister to the best of your abilities. The key is being open, being dependent, and being available to the Holy Spirit.

This idea is what caused me to develop a concept of pastoral care called ministry between miracles. We do not control miracles, but we leave the possibility for miracles open without increasing false hope. We depend on the Holy Spirit to take care of that aspect, and we do responsible and skillful ministry in the meantime.

I came to this conclusion as a result of my own educational and ministry experiences. From a Pentecostal parsonage in India I went to attend Yale University Divinity School. In India, I saw what the Spirit could do in a difficult situation. I learned at Yale what ministry can accomplish through learning and training. I began to think about what might happen if these two streams could come together; empowerment of the Holy Spirit and true ministerial competence coming together for increased effectiveness. That is what I am advocating here. Learn the skills and give them to God; give your knowledge and skills to the Holy Spirit to produce great results. The results may not always be what we want or expect, but they will always be the best.

So I call you to seek the empowerment of the Holy Spirit. Open your life for a new dimension of the work of the Holy Spirit in you. Give your prayers, sermons, and rituals to the Holy Spirit. Let Him use them for God's glory, and you watch the results in amazement. When nothing unusual seems to happen, walk by faith, knowing that you have given your very best to God and His people.

A Call to Excellence

I tell potential theological students that there is a difference between butchers and neurosurgeons, even though both groups use knives. The butcher produces dead meat, whereas the surgeon produces healing and wholeness. There are ministries within the Christian community that can only be characterized as butcher ministries because sincere persons with good intentions sensed the call of God and went out to minister without adequate preparation, causing pain to others often not even knowing it. Although they lack theological preparation, ministerial formation, and pastoral skills, many of them believe their ministry is adequate just because they are able to draw a crowd. Unfortunately, many of their sheep are wounded and must escape through the back doors to seek healing from other ministers and counselors. God's Word is a double-edged sword, and in untrained hands it can be a dangerous weapon. Faith is the substance of things hoped for and the evidence of things not seen, but toxic faith is a killer.

We all recognize that schools do not make ministers; it is God who calls persons to ministry. But called persons must subject themselves to training in ministry. Billy Graham said that if he had his ministry to do all over again, he would make two changes: first, he would study three times as much as he had. "I have preached too much and studied too little," said Graham. Secondly, he would give more time to prayer.

In a letter Graham wrote to John R. W. Stott, he quoted Donald Grey Barnhouse, a well-known Philadelphia pastor: "If I had only three years to serve the Lord, I would spend two of them studying and preparing."[1] It took the disciples of Jesus three years of training to do ministry in the primitive world of two thousand years ago. It seems unlikely that less training could produce a competent minister for this complex information age.

I am grateful for the many pastors and leaders who attend seminaries to continue their education and training. They get to spend time with theological faculty and other ministers in a process that can only be characterized as iron sharpening iron. They are able to examine their theologies and ministry practices and improve their knowledge and skills. As a result, these individuals can implement their newly acquired ministerial skills in their churches. I have heard glowing testimonies of improved ministries from church members of pastors involved in post-ordination studies.

I want to conclude this book by calling all Christian ministers to a more excellent level of ministry. I wish to invite current theological students to seek this same degree of excellence in their future ministry and to prepare for it to the best of their abilities. Unfortunately, I have witnessed less than excellent ministry in many parts of the world. While many faithful ministers of the gospel hold a very high standard for themselves, there are also ministers who preach unprepared sermons, teach superficial lessons, neglect the healing ministry of Jesus, and provide weak leadership. I have observed substandard ministries in both small churches and megachurches alike. While small churches cite their lack of resources as an excuse for substandard ministry, megachurches attribute their weaknesses to the volume of members they serve. Nonetheless, the quality of ministry should be a matter of the minister's convictions, not the size of the church.

This book presented a multifaceted, biblical view of Spirit-filled ministry based on the ministry of Jesus and the apostles. We have reviewed the ministry recorded in the book of Acts in view of the challenges confronting the church and Christian ministers in the twenty-first century. It is a difficult task to translate the vital ministry of the apostolic age to our postmodern period. This can only be accomplished, as I have mentioned several times in this volume, with the help of the Holy Spirit and through His refreshing, renewing, and empowering presence.

In terms of the major tasks of ministry, God is looking for Spirit-filled preachers who will share His Word in their time and place. He is seeking people who can exegete the Word and the world. Spirit-led preachers are capable of connecting the Word with the world in such a way that the Word impacts the inhabitants of that world. Even postmodernists seek a word from the Lord. Blessed are those who will hear that word from God and deliver it faithfully in the power of the Holy Spirit. I call ministers to excellence in preaching.

Good preaching must be complemented by outstanding teaching. The teaching ministry of the church determines the level of discipleship among its members. As Jesus preached the kingdom of God and taught the principles of kingdom lifestyle, we also must preach the good news and teach kingdom values in order to develop modern disciples. Only sound biblical teaching will motivate today's cultural Christians to grow in their faith and knowledge of the Lord Jesus Christ. God is seeking committed teachers who will inform and impart for the purpose of spiritual transformation, but the Holy Spirit is the supreme instructor. Good teachers must depend on the Holy Spirit for wisdom, revelation, and discernment. These Spirit-led teachers enable their students to experience the renewal of their minds and the transformation of their lives. I call ministers and educators to excellence in teaching.

Our broken world needs healers who move in the power of the Holy Spirit. Tired of self-help efforts and custom-made religions, people are seeking true healing for their shattered lives. Spirit-led ministers must offer them the healing power of Jesus, representing the body of Christ as an embodiment of a healing community. Pastors must involve church members in the healing ministry, so that all members of the body, not just ordained ministers, engage themselves in this healing work. Each member can be trained to minister healing in body, mind, spirit, and relationships. I call the church of Jesus Christ to excellence in healing ministry.

There is an international shortage of ethical leaders. It has become clear that this shortage is particularly acute in business, politics, and government. The church is also in need of Spirit-led servant leaders to guide her through the challenges of the current century. This need requires men and women in leadership who have encountered God and have experienced the anointing of the Holy Spirit. The body of Christ does not need tyrants or dictators; it needs apostles, prophets, evangelists, pastors, teachers, and other ministers who are led by the Spirit. I call Christian ministers to excellence in leadership.

As a minister of the gospel and an individual who trains Spirit-led ministers, I present this concern for excellence in ministry with much optimism because history attests that God always finds the human vessels He needs to fulfill His purposes in the world. Extraordinary individuals, such as Saint Paul, Saint Augustine, John Calvin, Martin Luther, and John Wesley, as well as ordinary persons such as Deacon Philip, John Mark, William Carey, William Seymour, and Mother Teresa were available to Him. God still wants to share the good news of Jesus Christ with the world. Those of us who are called to work with God on this project should consider ourselves truly blessed. May we give Him our very best, and may this be our prayer as we look into the future: Come, Holy Spirit! Come in your strength! Come in your power! Come and lead us!

Notes

Chapter 1

[1] H. Richard Niebuhr, *The Purpose of the Church and Its Ministry* (New York: Harper & Row, 1956), 64.
[2] David W. Bennett, *Metaphors of Ministry* (Grand Rapids: Baker, 1993), 53–54.
[3] David McKenna, *Renewing Our Ministry* (Waco: Word Books, 1986), 9.
[4] John W. Frye, *Jesus the Pastor* (Grand Rapids: Zondervan, 2000), 50–54.
[5] Stanley M. Burgess, *The Holy Spirit: Ancient Christian Traditions* (Peabody, MA: Hendrickson, 1997), 3.
[6] H. Richard Niebuhr, 66–74.
[7] Samuel Southard, *Pastoral Authority in Personal Relationships* (Nashville: Abingdon, 1969), 20–21.
[8] Ibid., 14.
[9] Eugene H. Peterson, *The Pastor: A Memoir* (New York: HarperOne, 2011).
[10] Henri Nouwen, *Creative Ministry* (Garden City, NY: Doubleday & Company, 1971).
[11] Victor Paul Furnish, "Theology and Ministry in the Pauline Letters," in *A Biblical Basis for Ministry*, ed. Earl E. Shelp and Ronald Sunderland (Philadelphia: Westminster Press, 1981), 128–136.
[12] Donald E. Messer, *Contemporary Images of Christian Ministry* (Nashville: Abingdon, 1989).
[13] William Willimon, *Pastor: The Theology and Practice of Ordained Ministry* (Nashville, Abingdon, 2000).

Chapter 2

[1] Charles A. Ver Straten, A Caring Church (Grand Rapids: Baker, 1988), 146.
[2] James F. Stitzinger, "Pastoral Ministry in History," in John A. MacArthur, Jr. (Ed.) *Rediscovering Pastoral Ministry* (Dallas: Word, 1995), 42.
[3] Thomas C. Oden, *Classical Pastoral Care*, 4 vols., (Grand Rapids: Baker, 1987).
[4] Oden, vol. 1, 13.
[5] Ibid., 13.
[6] Ibid., 42.
[7] Ibid., 43.
[8] Eddie Hyatt, *2000 Years of Charismatic Christianity* (Tulsa: Hyatt International Ministries, 1996).
[9] Oden, vol. 1, 149.
[10] Ibid., 160.
[11] Stitzinger, 52.
[12] Oden, vol. 2, 171.
[13] Oden, vol. 3, 28.
[14] Ibid., 200.
[15] Oden, vol. 4, 71.
[16] Stitzinger, 53.
[17] Winthrop S. Hudson, "The Ministry in the Puritan Age" in H. Richard Niebuhr and Daniel D. Williams, eds., *The Ministry in Historical Perspective* (San Francisco: Harper and Row, 1983), 199.
[18] Ibid., 194.
[19] Ibid., 196.
[20] William D. Salsbery, *Equipping and Mobilizing Believers to Perform a Shared Ministry of Pastoral Care*, D. Min. proj. (Tulsa: Oral Roberts University, 1991), 44.
[21] Niebuhr, 228.
[22] Sydney E. Mead, "The Rise of the Evangelical Conception of the Ministry in America: 1607–1850" in Niebuhr, 244.
[23] Robert S. Michaelsen, "Protestant Ministry in America: 1850–1950" in Niebuhr, 250.

[24] William A. Clebsch and Charles R. Jaekle, *Pastoral Care in Historical Perspective* (New York: Jason Aronson, 1975), 32–66.

[25] Howard Clinebell, *Basic Types of Pastoral Care & Counseling* (Nashville: Abingdon, 1984), 9, 17.

[26] Carrie Doehring, *The Practice of Pastoral Care: A Postmodern Approach* (Louisville, KY: Westminster John Knox Press, 2006).

[27] Karen D. Scheib, *Pastoral Care: Telling the Stories of Our Lives* (Nashville: Abingdon Press, 2016).

[28] Deborah van Deusen Hunsinger, *Bearing the Unbearable: Trauma, Gospel, and Pastoral Care* (Grand Rapids: William B. Eerdmans Publishing Company, 2015).

[29] Joseph C. Hough, Jr. and John B. Cobb, Jr., *Christian Identity and Theological Education* (Chicago: Scholars Press, 1985), 5–6.

[30] H. Richard Niebuhr, *The Purpose of the Church and Its Ministry* (New York: Harper & Row, 1956), 51.

Chapter 3

[1] Henri Nouwen, *The Wounded Healer* (Garden City, NY: Doubleday, 1979).

[2] Abraham Maslow, *Motivation and Personality* (New York: Harper & Row, 1970), 35–47.

[3] Erla Zwingle, "A World Together," National *Geographic* (August 1999), 28.

[4] Robert Coleman, *The Masterplan of Discipleship* (Grand Rapids: Baker, 1998).

[5] Charles V. Gerkin, *An Introduction to Pastoral Care* (Nashville: Abingdon, 1997).

[6] Peter Wagner, *Your Church Can Grow* (Glendale: Regal Books, 1976).

[7] Earl E. Shelp and Ronald H. Sunderland, eds., *Pastor as Priest* (New York: Pilgrim Press, 1987).

Chapter 4

[1] Herbert Anderson, The Family and Pastoral Care (Philadelphia: Fortress, 1989), 35–39.

2. Peter Martin, *A Marital Therapy Manual* (New York: Brunner/Mazel, 1976), 15–33.
3. Anderson, 83–106.
4. Christie Cozad Neuger, "Pastoral Counseling With Women," *Clergy Journal* 71, no. 1 (1994): 5–8.
5. Duane Parker, "Executive Director Notes," *Association of Clinical Pastoral Education News* (October, 1989): 3–4.
6. Kay Marshall Storm, *Women in Crisis* (Michigan: Ministry Resource Library, 1986).
7. Andrew Lester, *Pastoral Care with Children in Crisis* (Philadelphia: Westminster, 1985).
8. Robert T. Frerichs, "A History of the Continuing Education Movement," *The Drew Gateway* 47, no. 1 (1976–77): 1–9.
9. James Berkley, "The Unfinished Pastor," *Leadership* 5, no. 4 (1984): 128–129.
10. Connolly C. Gamble, Jr., "Continuing Education for Ministry: Perspectives and Prospects," *The Drew Gateway* 47, no. 1 (1976–77): 10-19. And "Continuing Education: The Contemporary Scene," *The Drew Gateway* 47, no. 1 (1976–77): 37–47.
11. Charles B. Fortier, "A Study of Continuing Education Needs of Clergymen in Lafayette Parish, Louisiana" (Doctoral Dissertation, Louisiana State University, 1972), *Dissertation Abstract International* 33, no.12A, 6589.
12. Donald Emler, "Mid-career Development of United Methodist Parish Ministers within the State University System of Continuing Education," (Doctoral Dissertation, Indiana University, 1973), *Dissertation Abstract International* 3, no. 08, 4555.
13. Jimmy W. Walker, "The Relationship of Continuing Professional Education and Pastoral Tenure among Southern Baptist Pastors," (Doctoral Dissertation, Texas State University, 1986), *Dissertation Abstract International* 47, no. 08A, 2855.
14. Thomson K. Mathew, "Development and Validation of an Instrument to Measure the Continuing Education Needs of Professional Chaplains" (Ed.D. diss., Oklahoma State Univ., 1992).

Chapter 5

1. William Hendriksen, New Testament Commentary: The Gospel of Luke, (Baker Book House, 1981), 351.
2. William Willimon, *Pastor: The Theology and Practice of Ordained Ministry* (Nashville, Abingdon, 2000), 77.
3. Aldwin Ragoonath, *How Shall They Hear?* (North Brunswick, NJ: Bridge-Logos, 1996), 4.
4. Ralph G. Turnbull, *A History of Preaching*, vol. 3 (Grand Rapids: Baker, 1976), 163–171.
5. Gerhard Friedrich, ed., *Theological Dictionary of the New Testament*, vol. 6 (Grand Rapids: W. B. Eerdmans, 1968), 781–862.
6. Ragoonath, 63-88.
7. Gijsbert D. J. Dingemans, "A Hearer in the Pew: Homiletical Reflections and Suggestions," in *Preaching as a Theological Task: A Collection of Essays in Honor of George Buttrick*, eds. Thomas G. Long and Ed Farley (Louisville: Westminster, 1996), 38–49.
8. Bill Easum, "Ancient Mission in the Contemporary World," *Circuit Rider*, July/August 2002, 24–26.
9. Rick Warren, "A Primer on Preaching Like Jesus," *REV*, March/April 2002, 45–50.
10. Tim Timmons, "Preaching to Convince," ed. James D. Berkley (Waco: Word, 1986), 20; quoted in Calvin Miller, *Market Place Preaching* (Grand Rapids: Baker, 1995), 18–19.
11. Edwin C. Dargon, *A Brief History of Great Preaching*, vol. 1 (New York: Burt Franklin, 1968), 37.
12. David Martyn Lloyd-Jones, *Studies in the Sermon on the Mount*, vol. 2 (Grand Rapids: W.B. Eerdmans, 1962), vii.
13. Zach Eswine, *Preaching to a Post-Everything World: Crafting Biblical Sermons That Connect with Our Culture* (Grand Rapids: Baker Books, 2008), 51–56.
14. Dennis F. Kinlaw, *Preaching in the Spirit* (Grand Rapids: Francis Asbury Press, 1985), 11.
15. Jacqueline Grey, *Three's A Crowd: Pentecostalism, Hermeneutics, and the Old Testament* (Eugene, OR: Pickwick Publications, 2011).

[16] Richard Lischer, *The End of Words: The Language of Reconciliation in a Culture of Violence* (Grand Rapids: William B. Eerdmans, 2005), 68.
[17] Ibid.

Chapter 6
[1] Lawrence Richards, *You, the Teacher* (Chicago: Moody Press, 1972), 66–67.
[2] Ronald G. Held, *Learning Together* (Springfield: Gospel Publishing House, 1976), 34.
[3] Leonard Sweet, *Postmodern Pilgrims: First Century Passion for the Twenty-first Century Church* (Nashville: Broadman & Holman, 2000).
[4] Malcolm S. Knowles, *Self-Directed Learning* (New York: Cambridge Book Company, 1988), 19.
[5] Ibid., 59–63.
[6] Benjamin Bloom, *Taxonomy of Educational Objectives* (New York: Longman, Green, and Co., 1956).
[7] Raymond Wlodkowski, *Enhancing Adult Motivation to Learn* (San Francisco: Jossey-Bass, 1988).
[8] Richard Paul and Linda Elder, *A Miniature Guide for Those Who Teach on How to Improve Student Learning* (Dillon Beach, CA: Foundation for Critical Thinking, 2002).
[9] Carnegie S. Calian, *The Ideal Seminary* (Louisville: Westminster John Knox Press, 2001), 37.

Chapter 7
[1] William A. Clebsch and Charles R. Jaekle, Pastoral Care in Historical Perspective (New York: Jason Aronson, 1975).
[2] Thomas C. Oden, *Classical Pastoral Care*, 4 vols. (Grand Rapids: Baker, 1987).
[3] Thomson K. Mathew, *Ministry Between Miracles* (Fairfax: Xulon, 2002).
[4] William Hulme, *Pastoral Care and Counseling* (Minneapolis: Augsburg, 1981).

Chapter 8
1. Bruce Goettsche, Principles of Effective Christian Leadership [online]; available from http://www.unionchurch.com/archive/050398.html.
2. Warren G. Bennis and Burt Nanus, *Leaders: The Strategy for Taking Charge* (New York: Harper, 1997).
3. Robert Webber, *The Younger Evangelicals: Facing the Challenges of the New World* (Grand Rapids: Baker, 2002).
4. Edward Bratcher, *Walk on Water Syndrome* (Grand Rapids: Word, 1984).
5. Gordon Fee, *Gospel and Spirit* (Peabody: Hendrickson, 1991), 120–143.
6. Oral Roberts, *Expect A Miracle* (Nashville: Thomas Nelson, 1995).
7. Edward Bratcher, *Walk on Water Syndrome* (Grand Rapids: Word, 1984).
8. John Kotter, *Leading Change* (Boston: Harvard Business School Press, 1996).
9. Kenneth O. Gangel, *Feeding and Leading* (Wheaton: Scripture Press, 1989), 189.
10. John Lawyer and Neil Katz, *Communication Skills for Ministry* (Dubuque: Kendall/ Hunt, 1983), 37–38.
11. J. Robert Clinton, *The Making of a Leader* (Colorado Springs: NavPress, 1988).
12. Henri Nouwen, *The Wounded Healer* (Garden City: Image Books, 1979).

Chapter 9
1. John Stott, Between Two Worlds (Grand Rapids: W.B. Eerdmans, 1982), 181.

Bibliography

Anderson, Herbert. *The Family and Pastoral Care.* Philadelphia: Fortress, 1989.

Anderson, Leith. *Dying for Change.* Minneapolis: Bethany House, 1990.

Bennis, Warren G., and Burt Nanus. *Leaders: The Strategy for Taking Charge.* New York: Harper, 1997. *Dissertation Abstract International* 33, no.12A, 6589.

Berkley, James. "The Unfinished Pastor." *Leadership* 5, no. 4 (1984): 128–129.

Bloom, Benjamin S. *Taxonomy of Educational Objectives.* New York: Longman, Green, and Co., 1956.

Bratcher, Edward. *Walk on Water Syndrome.* Grand Rapids: Word, 1984.

Burgess, Stanley M. *The Holy Spirit: Ancient Christian Traditions.* Peabody, MA: Hendrickson, 1997.

Calian, Carnegie S. *The Ideal Seminary.* Louisville: Westminster John Knox Press, 2001.

Clebsch, William A., and Charles R. Jaekle. *Pastoral Care in Historical Perspective.* New York: Jason Aronson, 1975.

Clinebell, Howard. *Basic Types of Pastoral Care & Counseling.* Nashville: Abingdon, 1984.

Clinton, J. Robert. *The Making of a Leader.* Colorado Springs: NavPress, 1988.

Coleman, Robert. *The Masterplan of Discipleship*. Grand Rapids: Baker, 1998.

Dargon, Edwin C. *A Brief History of Great Preaching*. Vol. 1. New York: Burt Franklin, 1968.

Dingemans, Gijsbert D. J. "A Hearer in the Pew: Homiletical Reflections and Suggestions." In *Preaching as a Theological Task: A Collection of Essays in Honor of George Buttrick*, ed. Thomas G. Long and Ed Farley, 38–49. Louisville: Westminster, 1996.

Doehring, Carrie. *The Practice of Pastoral Care: A Postmodern Approach*. Louisville, KY: Westminster John Knox Press, 2006.

Easum, Bill. "Ancient Mission in the Contemporary World." *Circuit Rider*, July/August 2002, 24–26.

Emler, Donald. "Mid-Career Development of United Methodist Parish Ministers Within the State University System of Continuing Education." Ph.D. diss., Indiana University, 1973. In *Dissertation Abstract International* 3, no. 8, 4555.

Erikson, Erik. *Identity: Youth and Crisis*. New York: W.W. Norton & Company, 1968.

Eswine, Zach. *Preaching to a Post-Everything World: Crafting Biblical Sermons That Connect with Our Culture*. Grand Rapids: Baker Books, 2008.

Fee, Gordon. *Gospel and Spirit*. Peabody: Hendrickson, 1991.

Fisher, David. *The Twenty-First Century Pastor*. Grand Rapids: Zondervan, 1996.

Fortier, Charles B. "A Study of Continuing Education Needs of Clergymen in Lafayette Parish, Louisiana." PhD diss., Louisiana State University, 1972. In *Dissertation Abstract International* 33, no 12A, 6589.

Frerichs, Robert T. "A History of the Continuing Education Movement." *The Drew Gateway* 47, no. 1 (1976–77): 1–9.

Friedrich, Gerhard, ed. *Theological Dictionary of the New Testament*, Vol. 6. Grand Rapids: W.B. Eerdmans, 1968.

Gamble, Connolly C., Jr. "Continuing Education for Ministry: Perspectives and Prospects." *The Drew Gateway* 47, no. 1 (1976–77): 10–19.

———. "Continuing Education: The Contemporary Scene." *The Drew Gateway* 47, no. 1 (1976–77): 37–47.

Gangel, Kenneth O. *Feeding and Leading*. Wheaton: Scripture Press, 1989.

Gerkin, Charles V. *An Introduction to Pastoral Care*. Nashville: Abingdon, 1997.

Goettsche, Bruce. *Principles of Effective Christian Leadership*. [online]; available from http://www.unionchurch.com/archive/050398.html.

Grey, Jacqueline. *Three's A Crowd: Pentecostalism, Hermeneutics, and the Old Testament*. Eugene, OR: Pickwick Publications, 2011.

Held, Ronald G. *Learning Together*. Springfield: Gospel, 1976.

Hendrickson, William. *New Testament Commentary: The Gospel of Luke*. Grand Rapids: Baker Book House, 1981, 351.

Hulme, William. *Pastoral Care and Counseling*. Minneapolis: Augsburg, 1981.

Hunsinger, Deborah van Deusen. *Bearing the Unbearable: Trauma, Gospel, and Pastoral Care*. Grand Rapids: William B. Eerdmans Publishing Company, 2015.

Hyatt, Eddie. *2000 Years of Charismatic Christianity*. Tulsa, OK: Hyatt International Ministries, 1996.

Kinlaw, Dennis F. *Preaching in the Spirit*. Grand Rapids: Francis Asbury Press, 1985.

Knowles, Malcolm S. *Self-Directed Learning*. Englewood Cliffs, NJ: Prentice Hall Regents, 1975.

Kotter, John. *Leading Change*. Boston: Harvard Business School Press, 1996.

Lawyer, John, and Neil Katz. *Communication Skills for Ministry.* Dubuque: Kendall/Hunt, 1983.

Lester, Andrew. *Pastoral Care With Children in Crisis.* Philadelphia: Westminster, 1985.

Lischer, Richard. *The End of Words: The Language of Reconciliation in a Culture of Violence.* Grand Rapids: Eerdmans, 2005.

Lloyd-Jones, David Martyn. *Studies in the Sermon on the Mount,* Vol. 2. Grand Rapids: W. B. Eerdmans, 1962.

MacArthur, John A., Jr. *Rediscovering Pastoral Ministry.* Dallas: Word, 1995.

Martin, Peter. *A Marital Therapy Manual.* New York: Brunner/Mazel, 1976.

Maslow, Abraham. *Motivation and Personality.* New York: Harper & Row, 1970.

Mathew, Thomson K. *Ministry Between Miracles.* Fairfax: Xulon, 2002.

Mathew, Thomson K. "Development and Validation of an Instrument to Measure the Continuing Education Needs of Professional Chaplains." Ed.D. diss., Oklahoma State University, 1992.

Mead, Sydney E. "The Rise of the Evangelical Conception of the Ministry in America: 1607–1850." In *The Ministry in Historical Perspective,* ed. H. Richard Niebuhr and Daniel D. Williams, 207–249. San Francisco: Harper and Row, 1983.

Messer, Donald E. *Contemporary Images of Christian Minister.* Nashville: Abingdon, 1989.

Michaelsen, Robert S. "Protestant Ministry in America: 1850-1950," In *The Ministry in Historical Perspective,* ed. H. Richard Niebuhr and Daniel D. Williams, 250–288. San Francisco: Harper and Row, 1983.

Neuger, Christie Cozad. "Pastoral Counseling with Women." *Clergy Journal* 71, no. 1 (1994): 5–8.

Niebuhr, H. Richard, and Daniel D. Williams, eds. *The Ministry in Historical Perspective.* San Francisco: Harper and Row, 1983.

Nouwen, Henri. *The Wounded Healer.* Garden City: Image Books, Doubleday, 1979.

Oden, Thomas C. *Classical Pastoral Care.* Vol. 1. Grand Rapids: Baker, 1987.

_____. *Classical Pastoral Care.* Vol. 2. Grand Rapids: Baker, 1987.

_____. *Classical Pastoral Care.* Vol. 3. Grand Rapids: Baker, 1987.

_____. *Classical Pastoral Care.* Vol. 4. Grand Rapids: Baker, 1987.

Ortiz, Juan Carlos. *Disciple.* Carol Stream, IL: Creation House, 1975.

Parker, Duane. "Executive Director Notes." *Association of Clinical Pastoral Education News* (October 1989): 3–4.

Paul, Richard, and Linda Elder. *A Miniature Guide for Those Who Teach on How to Improve Student Learning.* United States of America: Foundation for Critical Thinking.

Peterson, Eugene H. *The Pastor: A Memoir.* New York: HarperOne, 2011.

Pruyser, Paul. *The Minister as Diagnostician.* Philadelphia: Westminster, 1976.

Ragoonath, Aldwin. *How Shall They Hear?* North Brunswick, NJ: Bridge-Logos, 1996.

Richards, Lawrence. *You, the Teacher.* Chicago: Moody Press, 1972.

Roberts, Oral. *Expect a Miracle.* Nashville: Thomas Nelson, 1995.

Salsbery, William D. "Equipping and Mobilizing Believers to Perform a Shared Ministry of Pastoral Care." D.Min. diss., Oral Roberts University, 1991.

Sanford, John A. *Ministry Burnout.* New York: Paulist, 1982.

Karen D. Scheib. *Pastoral Care: Telling the Stories of Our Lives.* Nashville: Abingdon Press, 2016.

Shelp, Earl E., and Ronald H. Sunderland, eds. *Pastor as Priest.* New York: Pilgrim Press, 1987.

Stitzinger, James F. "Pastoral Ministry in History." In *Rediscovering Pastoral Ministry*, ed. John A. MacArthur, Jr. Dallas: Word, 1995.

Storm, Kay Marshall. *Women in Crisis*. Michigan: Ministry Resource Library, 1986.

Stott, John. *Between Two Worlds*. Grand Rapids: W. B. Eerdmans, 1982.

Sweet, Leonard. *Postmodern Pilgrims: First Century Passion for the Twenty-First Century Church*. Nashville: Broadman & Holman, 2000.

Timmons, Tim. "Preaching to Convince." ed. James D. Berkley. Waco: Word, 1986. Quoted in Calvin Miller, *Market Place Preaching*, 18–19, Grand Rapids: Baker, 1995.

Turnbull, Ralph G. *A History of Preaching*, Vol. 3. Grand Rapids: Baker, 1976.

Ver Straten, Charles A. *A Caring Church*. Grand Rapids: Baker, 1988.

Walker, Jimmy W. "The Relationship of Continuing Professional Education and Pastoral Tenure among Southern Baptist Pastors." PhD diss., Texas State University, 1986. In *Dissertation Abstract International* 47, no. 08A, 2855.

Webber, Robert. *The Younger Evangelicals: Facing the Challenges of the New World*. Grand Rapids: Baker, 2002.

Wagner, Peter. *Your Church Can Grow*. Glendale: Regal Books, G/L Publications, 1976.

Warren, Rick. "A Primer on Preaching Like Jesus." *REV* March/April 2002, 45–50.

Willimon, William. *Pastor: The Theology and Practice of Ordained Ministry*. Nashville: Abingdon, 2000.

Wlodkowski, Raymond. *Enhancing Adult Motivation to Learn*. San Francisco: Jossey-Bass, 1988.

Zwingle, Erla. "A World Together." *National Geographic* 196, August 1999, 12–33.

Printed in the USA
CPSIA information can be obtained
at www.ICGtesting.com
LVHW042016300823
756752LV00001B/16

9 781512 792317